'One cannot too highly recommend this informative book, in which can be found all the ways and means to enjoy bird life, and at the same time help the wild birds and other small creatures . . . enchanting reading . . .' *The Animal World*

'Although primarily a work of reference it is also a book to read for sheer enjoyment' *Bird Notes*

'A superlative delight to all bird lovers' *Christian Herald*

'Packed with fascinating information' *Woman's Realm*

'Intensely practical, always pleasant to read . . . covers a far wider field than its title suggests' *Countryside*

'Excellent . . . a kind of ornithological good-food-homes-and-gardens guide soundly based on Tony Soper's practical experience and salted with a genial humour which Robert Gillmor's witty drawings exactly match' *The Times Literary Supplement*

TONY SOPER has a number of successful television wildlife documentaries and expeditions to his credit. In the BBC he helped to create the famous Natural History Unit with Desmond Hawkins. Now, as a freelance naturalist, film producer and qualified Master Diver, he spends most of his life working amongst the animals of the sea-shore and estuaries of his native West Country.

THE BIRD TABLE BOOK

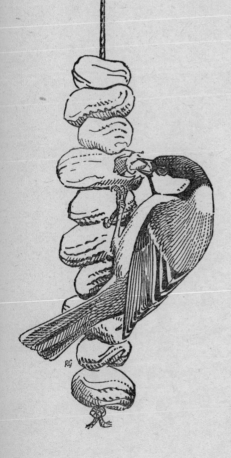

THE BIRD

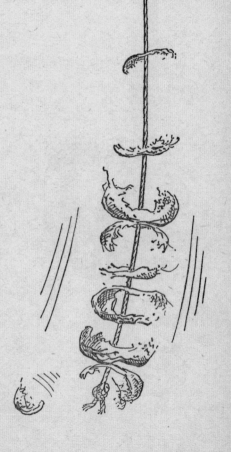

TONY SOPER

TABLE BOOK

Illustrations by Robert Gillmor

PAN BOOKS LTD : LONDON

First published 1965 by David & Charles Ltd.

This edition published 1968 by Pan Books Ltd.,
33 Tothill Street, London, S.W.1

330 02197 4

Unabridged

FOR RAE

Printed in Great Britain by
Cox & Wyman Ltd., London, Reading and Fakenham

Contents

PREFACE   11

1   The bird garden   13
2   Water   19
3   Nest sites and nestboxes   27
4   The bird table   41
5   Predators and poisons   57
6   Why only birds?   63
7   Species notes   69

APPENDICES

A   Recipes and bird food supplies   99
B   Suppliers of bird furniture   101
C   Birds which visit feeding stations   104
D   Birds which use nestboxes   105
E   Life-spans of wild birds   106
F   Treatment of casualties   108
G   Organizations   110
H   Birds and the law   112
I   Birdsong recordings   113

BIBLIOGRAPHY   115

ACKNOWLEDGEMENTS   117

INDEX   119

Illustrations

MAIN TEXT FIGURES

Structure of feathers   20
Blackbird oiling   20
Dustbin lid bird bath   21
Wren post in pond   24
Anting starlings   25
Crotch-site pruning   28
Enclosed and open nestboxes   33
Details of nestbox construction   35
Hard and soft bills   42
Habitats   46
Nut skewer   50
Suet stick   51
Bird table dimensions   55
Hedgehog nest box   65
Kestrel box   71
Bird furniture   101-3

PHOTOGRAPHS

Family of blue tits at bird bath (Eric Hosking)
Hen blackbird bathing (Eric Hosking)
Spotted flycatcher collecting nest material
    (Eric Hosking)
Blackbird's nest in wing of car (L. G. Charrett)
Blackbird's nest on tool bag (William S. Paton)
Wren's nest in coil of rope (William S. Paton)
Marsh tit at nestbox (Eric Hosking)
Great spotted woodpecker feeding from
    the hand (Michael Wilkinson)
House martins collecting mud (Eric Hosking)
Young robins (John Markham)
Nuthatch at post feeding station (John Markham)
Great tit feeding from the hand (Eric Hosking)
Robin's nest in pitcher (Eric Hosking)
Robin in snow (Eric Hosking)
Myrtle warbler on bird table (E. H. Ware)

Preface

The object of this book is to suggest ways in which we may have the interest and pleasure of sharing our lives with wild birds. Our working area need not necessarily be a spacious and old-established garden. Most of us have access to a window-sill and this can be one of the most entertaining bird locations.

Even the vicinity of offices and industrial premises can be successfully adapted to bird gardening. Very often these places are already natural sanctuaries, guarded by high fences and impenetrable to small boys and cats. They need only a few of the right bushes and some open water to stimulate a bird take-over bid. In these enlightened days new civic and commercial enterprises often surround their buildings with soothing gardens and reflective ponds. How much more attractive they will be with the added pleasures of natural colour, movement and song provided by wild birds. With only a little foresight at the planning stage, a potentially unsuitable bird garden can be transformed into a thriving nature reserve, to the benefit of staff and, perhaps, output as well.

Although it is true that ill-conceived commercial and residential development places great strains on wildlife many species have undoubtedly adapted themselves to peaceful co-existence with man. If we provide the right facilities we may expect to encourage new and ever more exciting species to regard us as sources of food and shelter, rather than as enemies. So let us make our gardens, our city centres and our factory grounds attractive places for birds as well as for ourselves. The two objects are perfectly compatible.

1 *The bird garden*

An open well-kept lawn is almost essential to a bird garden. It gives a clear view and makes a happy hunting area for birds searching for ants, cockchafer grubs and worms. Worms are much misunderstood creatures and it certainly is a mistake to try to kill them off. They are useful, they aerate and fertilize the soil, and though wormcasts may be unsightly they consist of fine rich soil. Spread them with a lawn rake or drag a weighted piece of wire netting over them before mowing. In the autumn, don't be too quick to sweep up the fallen leaves. Worms like leaves (especially willow and cherry), and birds like worms.

The bird garden should have a varied terrain, with changes of level, corners, miniature cliffs, valleys, hills, ravines, and low drystone walls – all features which will provide a diversity of insect life and rich foraging areas. Flower-beds and neat borders do not offer much of interest, and an over-tidy garden is an unexciting hunting-ground. Try to organize a rock bank or low wall in a warm or south-facing part of the garden, so that it is less likely to be snowed up in winter. A reasonable amount of 'jungle', plenty of berry-bearing

trees and shrubs, and a good lawn, are the important things
to aim for. Incidentally, if you are having a new house built,
be very careful that the builders set the topsoil aside for
subsequent replacement before they start crashing about
with bulldozers. Builders are all too ready to bury your vital
topsoil under tons of useless subsoil, and you will find it is
a long uphill grind to produce a fertile garden.

The best bird-garden boundary ever devised is the Devon
hedgerow. A wide foundation-bank with rough stone and
greenery, with ivy and ferns and wild flowers growing out of
it, and topped with a close hawthorn or hazel hedge, is a
bird paradise. One of the many beauties of a hedgerow is
that it provides a variety of food in winter time when natural
resources are at their lowest. Thrushes will eat berry-pulp
and pass the pips. Then the finches and tits will eat the pips
as they forage along the hedgerow bottom. Dead leaves and
debris shelter hibernating flies and insects, spiders, woodlice
and centipedes, all of which are good for wrens, tits, and
dunnocks. In the hedge itself, the leaves stay attached and
provide warmth and cover through the winter. The bank
harbours yet more grubs and insects, wintering aphids, and
their eggs, chrysalids, and so on. Common hedgerow birds
are blackbird, thrush, chaffinch, yellow-hammer, dunnock,
robin, wren, whitethroat, linnet, great tit, blue tit, long-
tailed tit, and willow warbler. One of the most distressing
country sights nowadays is the bulldozing of hedgerows in
order to make bigger and yet bigger fields to increase pro-
ductive acreage.

If you haven't the space to develop a Devon hedgerow,
then a thorn, holly or hazel hedge will do very well instead.
Put a couple of crab-apple trees in it: they will provide
useful stand-by food supplies in hard weather. Fieldfares
will hack open the apples, and chaffinches will eat the pips.

Generally speaking, it is as well to avoid planting coarse
thick-leaved evergreens. The rhododendrons and laurels
beloved of town councils are unpromising bird habitats,
taking light from the ground and not offering many insects
in return. If you have lots of room then you might plant an

isolated group of pine or larch in the hope of attracting goldcrests and crossbills. But have *some* evergreens, because they provide autumn and winter cover for roosting birds. A berry-bearing holly will serve a double purpose. Have one tall tree at least, a poplar for instance, and your thrush will sing from the topmost branch.

If you are lucky enough to have some old fruit trees, keep one or two for the birds. Leave the fruit on them and it will be welcomed by thrushes, fieldfares and redwings in the winter. Tits are also worth encouraging in orchards because they decimate the bug population. And if you make sure there is a plentiful water supply, they may eat less of your fruit.

BERRY-BEARING TREES AND SHRUBS

YEW. *Taxus baccata*. Evergreen. As a tree it may grow exceptionally to ninety feet, but as a bush of only six feet or so it makes a good hedge and provides nesting-sites. Slow growing, it may be fifteen years before it fruits and it may live for 2,000 years. A very good bird tree, the fleshy red berries are favourites with thrushes and starlings. The birds eat the pulp, but pass the poisonous seed without harm. Yew foliage and bark are also poisonous.

HAZEL. *Corylus avellana*. Deciduous bush, branching from the ground and growing to fifteen feet. Prefers rich soil, not too wet. Useful as hedgerow plant although it doesn't provide good nest sites (good pea sticks though). Nut harvest in August/September.

BARBARY (Common barbary). *Berberis vulgaris*. Deciduous. Grows thickly branched to five or six feet. The coral-red berries have a high vitamin C content and are eaten by most birds, particularly blackbirds. Cultivated species and varieties: *B. darwinii*, evergreen, is the commonest form, growing to about ten feet. Purple fruit. Can be planted as

hedge; *B. aggregata* Buccaneer, deciduous, has long-lasting berries and grows to nine feet; *B. wilsonæ*, deciduous, translucent coral berries. All the Barbarys are easy to grow and provide thick cover and weed-free ground underneath them.
COTONEASTER. *Cotoneaster integerrima*. Useful because it fruits late, after the hawthorn and before the ivy harvest. Thrushes, blackbirds, finches and tits like its rich red berries. Grows almost anywhere. Cultivated forms come in a wide

variety, from a few inches to twenty-five feet in height. *C. dammeri* and *C. prostrata* are trailers, small but ever-spreading; *C. buxifolia*, *C. francheti* and *C. lactea* are evergreen wall-climbers, growing to five, ten and fifteen feet, respectively; *C. horizontalis* and *C. rotundifolia* are deciduous, and grow to about four feet, with fan-like branches. *C. simonsii* makes an effective hedge, and produces good berries.

HAWTHORN (or Whitethorn). *Crataegus monogyna*. Makes excellent boy-proof hedge and grows almost anywhere. Blackbirds, fieldfares, and redwings all love the scarlet haws. Do not confuse this tree with the blackthorn, whose sloes are not much liked by birds.

ROWAN (Mountain Ash). *Sorbus aucuparia*. A top-class bird tree, not fussy about soil but it needs light. Grows fifteen to twenty-five feet and spreads. Mistle thrushes are very fond of the bunches of brilliant coral-red fruit. Fruits in August. Every Highland croft used to be surrounded by rowans, because the tree was supposed to have magic powers and guard against evil. *Sorbus vilmorinii* is a Chinese species which bears big berries and only grows to twelve feet.

HOLLY. *Ilex aquifolium*. Makes an excellent evergreen hedge. Thrushes and starlings like the berries, but these only come freely from an unclipped plant. Hollies are either male or female, and only the female produces berries. They also tend to be difficult to grow, so it may be best to buy from a nurseryman, when you can be sure of getting a strong female.

There must be one male somewhere near, of course, for cross-fertilization. Otherwise, plant several and hope for the best. The cultivated forms are the more reliable. *I.* Golden King is a small holly reaching to ten feet and bearing a good berry crop. *I.* Madame Briot grows to eighteen feet and bears golden berries.

SPINDLE. *Euonymus europaeus.* A bushy and ornamental shrub, growing to fifteen feet. Prefers chalk or lime-rich soil. Pink and orange fruit and beautiful autumn colours.

LIME (Linden). *Tilia cordata.* A large tree, growing exceptionally to 150 feet, but very amenable to pruning. One of the few forest trees to be pollinated by insects. There is a species of aphid which prefers lime trees, and exudes a sticky honey-dew which attracts insects, especially bees, so that limes are humming with insect sounds and movement in summer. Birds come for the insects in summer, and for the fruits in autumn.

IVY. *Hedera helix.* Good birdman's plant, which climbs or carpets the ground, but only flowers when it reaches light. Very attractive to insects when it flowers in September/October, and useful to birds when it bears berries in May and June. Wrens roost in it. Destructive to trees and walls of course, but why not offer up a tree or an old wall as sacrifice?

ELDER. *Sambucus nigra.* Some gardeners think of elder as a weed, but the bird gardener grows it because tits and thrushes like the purple berries and the early leaves make good nesting cover. Fast grower and takes plenty of pruning punishment.

GUELDER ROSE. *Viburnum opulus.* Grows to eighteen feet, produces large, flat clusters of flowers and red berries. The cultivated variety, *V. compactum*, is useful for a small garden, as it can be kept to six feet. The species of Guelder Rose often sold as the Snowball Bush is sterile and useless for birds.

HONEYSUCKLE. *Lonicera periclymenum.* A liana which entwines and climbs trees or bushes, or any man-made framework, but is very strong and will distort a growing plant with its vigorous coils. The nectar is difficult to reach and only insects with long probosci, such as the privet hawk-moth, can get at it. Blackbirds, tits and warblers like the berries of the wild or cultivated forms.

There are, of course, plenty of other trees and bushes which produce bird berries and you may care to experiment. Fruit trees of all kinds are highly suitable, and your conscience may even allow you to take a certain amount for your own table.

Sunflowers, if left to seed, are irresistible to tits, nuthatches and finches, and may even entice goldcrests if you are lucky. Forget-me-nots and cornflowers also produce seeds which are attractive to finches. (At nesting time, goldfinches may gather bunches of forget-me-not flowers and use them as building materials.) Other useful birdseed plants are cosmos, china asters, scabious, evening primrose, antirrhinum and common field-poppy.

WEEDS

Many weeds produce seeds which are sought after by birds. Finches, for example, are keen on thistle. Knapweed, teazle, ragwort and nettles are all attractive to birds, if not to the human gardener. If you feel that deliberate weed-growing is asking rather too much, then I suggest you go on collecting expeditions and keep the seeds for bird-table use as described in a later chapter.

2 Water

Some birds can last a long time without drinking, some will die within a few days, but none can manage entirely without water, which is essential to the proper functioning of their bodies. Although birds do not sweat, they lose water, mainly by excretion, and must make up the loss. They will derive some water from their food, and the rest from drinking. Tree-living species may sip from foliage after rain, but most birds will visit ponds and streams. Some will fill their bills, then raise their heads to let the water run down their throats; some will keep their bills in the water; and some will sip from the surface of the water as they fly past. Swifts and swallows even bathe in flight, dipping under with a quick splash as they go by.

Birds also need water to help with the constant problem of keeping their plumage in order. Quite apart from the fact that feathers are a vital part of their flying apparatus, plumage acts as an insulator and regulates body temperature. To be fully efficient, the feathers must be kept in good condition, and feather maintenance looms large in a bird's life. Bathing is the first move in a complicated sequence of events.

The object of the bathe is to wet the plumage without actually soaking it (if the feathers become too wet they may deteriorate). Birds will sometimes bathe in light rain, but if they are caught out in a heavy downpour they will hunch into a special position, reaching upwards and tightening their feathers so that the rain pours off quickly.

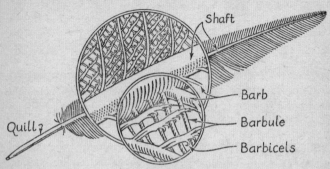

After the bath the bird will shake itself and begin 'oiling'. With the tail twisted to one side, it will reach down with its bill to collect fatty oil from its preen gland. Then, very carefully, it will rub the oil into the feathers, all over the

Blackbird - oiling

body. The difficult stage is when it wants to oil its head. To do this, it will use a foot, first oiling the foot and then scratching the grease on to the head. Next, comes the preening session, when the bird will nibble and stroke all its feathers. This may take a long time, and afterwards the bird will stretch and settle itself until its plumage is in full flying and insulating order – all systems go.

Unless you are lucky enough to have a stream or pond in your garden you will obviously have to provide water in some form or another. The bird bath is the obvious answer, although it is not the best. However, if you are short of space, it will suffice. The simplest version is an upturned dustbin lid, supported by three bricks or sunk into the ground, although if you sink it, it will be more difficult to keep ice-free in winter. An advantage of keeping it off the ground is that you are providing extra foraging ground and possibly a toad-hole underneath! The water level should vary from about one inch depth to not more than four inches, and it should have a shallow approach as most birds much prefer shallow water for bathing. Always use clean water and keep the bath up to its marks.

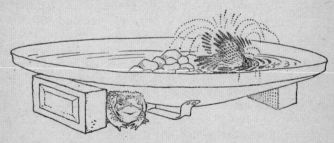

If you jib at introducing dustbin lids into your garden, use any similarly-shaped, shallow bowl, but beware of the ornamental, plastic, so-called 'bird baths' which garden shops sell and which may have a slippery slope leading to a cavernous well. Whatever kind of bowl you use, put it in shade and within reasonable range of cover and safety, but not so close that a cat may lurk and pounce. A point to remember is that birds get rather excited and preoccupied about their bathing; they tend, therefore, to be more vulnerable then than at other times.

At all times it is important to avoid letting the bath go dry, and it is especially important to keep it ice-free in winter. If the bowl is breakable, put a chunk of soft-wood into it so that if the water freezes the strain will be taken by the wood and not the bowl. I have seen a blue tit cracking a thin layer of ice, but this only served to show how badly it needed water. If your bath is a few inches off the ground, you can put one of those slow-burning night-lights underneath but, best of all, put an aquarium immersion heater in the pool, covered with some gravel. Connected to a thermostat (also submerged), it will control the water temperature so that there is a permanently ice-free area. Provided the mains lead is of a suitable outdoor type and the connections are properly made, no danger is involved. Both the immersion heater and the thermostat can be obtained from any aquarium dealer (or from Queensborough Fisheries, 111 Goldhawk Road, Shepherds Bush, London W12). These gadgets are very reliable, but if you want to be extra cautious get an electrician to wire *two* of the heaters in parallel. Then if one fails the other will still carry on.

Do *not* use glycerine, or anti-freeze of any kind, to keep the water ice-free. These chemicals will cause havoc to a bird's feathers at a time when they should be in first-class condition to keep out the cold. People sometimes ask why birds bath so much in freezing weather, and the answer must now be obvious. To keep warm, the feathers must be efficient, and to have efficient feathers the bird must go through the preening ritual which starts with a bath.

While a bird bath will serve its purpose quite adequately, a properly-stocked and regulated pool with oxygenating plants and fish is infinitely preferable, and much more rewarding. The water should be very shallow, but if you are going to make a special pond you may want to have a deeper section in which to raise fish in the hope of attracting kingfishers and herons. Design the pond so that there is a gently-shelving, shallow area leading to the main depth of eighteen inches or so. And provide a gently-sloping approach to the shallow area so that hedgehogs and grass snakes, and other welcome animals, can come to drink and bathe (and get out again!).

Now the easiest, and probably the best, plan is to make the pond-bed out of heavy-duty polythene lining (e.g. Butyl). The great advantage of this method is that you don't need to do any concreting. Make sure the lining has a generous overlap so that you can conceal the above-water parts by hiding them under turf or a dry-stone pond edging. If you prefer to make a concrete pool, be sure to seal the cement with a bituminous paint or water-seal cement. Put several inches of good soil in the bottom of the pond for anchoring aquatic plants. Fill carefully with water, either through a fine watering-rose or by putting a washing-up bowl in the pool and letting the water pour gently off its edges so that it does not churn up the soil.

It is essential to put in some oxygenating aquatic plants as these will absorb the carbon dioxide produced by all the water creatures which will colonize your pool, whether you like it or not. These plants are vital if you want to keep a healthy, smell-free pond. Get pest-free specimens from a nursery. The following plants can be recommended; all of them are oxygenating and will grow in three or four inches of soil covered by three to five inches of water:

Sagittaria graminea. This plant will also absorb all excreta from livestock in the pond as manure.

Callitriche autumnalis. Essential, as it retains oxygenating properties throughout winter.

Hottonia palustris. Water violet.

Isoetes lacustris. Quillwort. This is also an excellent food for fish.

Tillaea recurva.

Eleocharis acicularis.

Anchor these plants into the soil with strips of lead or stones, to give them a good start. To keep the sides of the pond clean, buy some common water snails from an aquarist. (The cheaper species will do the job just as well as the expensive ones.) If there is enough room have a small island in the middle but, in any case, fix a couple of small sticks in such a way that tits and wrens can hang on to them while they drink. The simplest method is to submerge a flower-pot upside down in the water and poke a stick through the hole.

In a week or so, when the plants have taken hold and the water has settled down and cleared, introduce some fish. Goldfish if you like, but why not stick to good British species like stickle-backs and minnows? Any of these will deal with the mosquito and gnat larvae which will try to colonize the pond. But don't overstock. A rough rule of thumb is that each inch of fish requires twenty-four square inches of surface area.

There are plenty of other creatures you can introduce, such as newts, frogs, water-spiders and beetles (but not great diving beetles – *Dytiscus marginalis* – because they are fierce and will attack fish much bigger than themselves). You will find that the finished product will give you as much pond-watching pleasure as it does the birds; and if, one day, a heron comes and eats your fish you must grin and bear it and re-stock the pond.

Unless your garden is on sandy ground, you may like to provide a dust bath for sparrows and wrens. The dusting-place should be well sheltered, with some cover nearby, and can consist of a couple of square feet of well-sifted sand, earth

and ash to a depth of a few inches. Sprinkle the dust-bath
with bug powder or spray (e.g. Cooper's Household Insect
Powder or Poultry Aerosol) every now and again, for the
common good. Birds will also sun-bathe, smoke-bathe, and
even bathe in ants, but the reasons for this behaviour are
not yet fully understood.

*Anting starlings -
like a group of
frenetic twisters-
drawn from frames of ciné film.*

3 Nest sites and nestboxes

Your bird visitors are now well-fed and watered, and the next move is to improve their nesting facilities. By their nature houses, outbuildings and gardens provide dozens of potential nest sites, although in these tidy-minded days we tend to build with fewer holes and corners. Very often, we can turn an uninviting building into a highly-desirable bird residence with the minimum of effort. Once again, we must bear in mind that different birds have different requirements, and while a blue tit will choose a secret place, entered by what seems an impossibly narrow hole, a swan will build a great mound of a nest and sit in state for all to see. In Devon now, we have the curious spectacle of herring gulls choosing to nest by the cottage chimney-pots of fishing villages. Soon after the young are hatched they wander about all over the rooftops.

We can divide birds roughly into those which nest in holes and those which do not. Tits, nuthatches and wood-peckers are hole-nesters; while flycatchers, robins, black-birds and thrushes live mostly on the open plan. All birds, no matter what type of nest they choose, need protection from their enemies and shelter from the elements if they are to thrive, so most of them build in cover of some kind.

NATURAL NEST SITES

Hedges are the most obvious places for nests. A good beech, holly, hawthorn or yew hedge contains dozens of likely building-sites and also provides a good defence barrier. It is important that there should be plenty of forks in the branches to provide a foundation for the first nest twigs. (Hazel makes a poor nesting tree because it offers so few fork sites.) By judicious pruning at about the five-foot height you can often turn an unpromising hedge into a likely attraction. Prune your hedge in early spring and autumn, leaving it undisturbed during the breeding season. When pruning fruit trees, make a crotch-site here and there in the body of the tree, in the hope of attracting a goldfinch to nest.

The berry-bearing shrubs often serve as nesting areas in the spring; if you have brambles and gorse in your garden, you may find they will harbour dunnocks or linnets. Honeysuckle seems to have a special attraction for flycatchers. Once a bird has chosen its nest site leave it to get on with the job. Don't try to help it with the construction, and don't 'improve' the situation, or it may desert. Don't fuss it!

A friend of mine who made an island on his pond was rewarded by having a pair of canada geese take it over. If you are lucky enough to have plenty of water, grow a lush area of wild celery, millet, reeds and sedges in clumps. If the reed-bed is large enough, you may get reed and sedge warblers, and possibly reed buntings, building in it.

Now for the hole-nesters. Naturally, they will prefer tree holes and it may be that you already have some old trees – fruit trees, perhaps – which have begun to decay in a manner attractive to birds. If not, you might consider introducing some holes into a decaying tree with a brace and bit. Start some promising holes of about one and a quarter inch diameter and a woodpecker may finish the job. If the woodpecker gives up, a nuthatch may take over and plaster the entrance hole with mud to suit its own preference. Or, you might try importing an old tree or tree trunk, complete with holes, and setting it up in a secluded position. At worst, you will end up with a pair of starlings. Personally, I like to have a pair of starlings nesting nearby because they are such entertaining vocalists and are remarkable mimics. We once had one that gave a first-class rendering of a hen that had just laid an egg, but the climax of its repertoire was a beautiful pussy-cat's miaow.

Making and enlarging holes is great fun, and when you have finished working on trees, you might turn your attentions to the walls of your house and outbuildings. Quite often it is possible to enlarge cracks so that there is the inch-and-an-eighth necessary for a tit to squeeze through. I am not suggesting you tear your house apart just for a few birds, but you will find plenty of likely and safe places if you look around, armed with a strong auger or jemmy. Try drilling some discreet one-and-a-quarter-inch holes in your garage doors. Make one entrance up near the roof and swallows may colonize the loft, although you will need to have a ceiling to protect the cellulose of your car from the droppings.

If you are building a garden wall, do not overdo the pointing; leave one or two gaps and you may attract a pied wagtail. Even grey wagtails take freely to man-provided nest sites in culvert and bridge stone-work. The height of the holes and cavities is not vitally important, although round about the five-foot mark is probably ideal. With a desirable site, birds will not be too choosey. Robins have nested at ground level and great tits as high as twenty-four feet, although these are exceptional instances. The holes should,

however, be in a sheltered position and facing somewhere within an arc drawn from north through east to south-east. Hot sun is bad, and so is an entrance facing into a cold wind.

An ancient, disintegrating stone wall is an asset to cherish and so is an old garden shed. The wall may be a haven for tits, nuthatches and wagtails, and the shed may be a thriving bird slum in no time at all if you develop it a little. Shelves around the walls and under the roof at different heights could provide homes for swallows, blackbirds and robins. A bundle of pea sticks in a corner may make a home for a wren. Leave an old tweed coat hanging up with a wide pocket gaping open for a robin. Keep the floor clear, though, to discourage rats. If necessary, put a rat-trap tunnel against the walls, but see that it does not let in light and attract ground birds. Make sure there is a good entrance hole somewhere, in case a bird is locked in by mistake.

On the outside of the shed grow a jungle of creeping ivy and honeysuckle. Hide a half-coconut (with a drain-hole in the bottom of the cup) in the creeper for a possible spotted flycatcher. Try excavating a nest cavity in the middle of a brushwood bundle and lean it against an outside wall. Lastly, lean an old plank against the dampest, darkest wall to make a haven for snails, and farm them on behalf of the thrushes.

MAN-MADE NEST SITES

There is good historical precedent for putting up bird houses (Noah must have had a dove-cote on top of the Ark). In Roman times there was a thriving pigeon 'fancy' with rooftop pigeon towns. Columbaria of differing architectural styles spread from Rome through Europe to Scotland and the rest of Britain through the centuries. The custom declined in the eighteenth century, when the introduction of root and clover crops made it possible to keep more cattle and sheep through the winter, thus providing fresh meat which made the pigeon 'squab' redundant. However, the tradition still flourishes, with thousands of elaborate lofts dedicated to the racing pigeon.

But the traditional man-provided nest is the robin's kettle, stuck five feet up in the fork of a tree. The kettle should be at least quart size, and the spout should point down so that rainwater can drain away. As an encouragement, prime the nest with some dead leaves or a plaited circle of straw.

The most unusual man-made nest site I ever saw was a birdcage, hanging high up on a cob wall in the village of Middle Wallop in Hampshire. It turned out that a hoopoe had reared young in a perfectly normal cavity-site in the wall, but one of the nest-  lings had fallen out of the hole a bit too soon. The villagers had hoisted up the bird- cage and left the door open, installing the unfortunate young bird inside. Incredibly, the adult hoopoe carried on feeding the baby as if nothing had happened, going in and out of the birdcage as if it were the most ordinary thing in the world. The story has a happy ending, too, because the whole family finally fledged successfully and flew off. But hoopoes are rare breeders in this country, so I am not going to suggest that we all invest in hoopoe birdcages.

Every year for some time past a pair of mute swans has tried to nest on a tidal sandbank near the mouth of the estuary at Newton Ferrers in South Devon. They seem unable to grasp the fact that Atlantic seawater rises and falls, and as fast as they build a nest the rising tide washes it away. The scientists of the International Paint Company, who have a research station nearby, came to the rescue, constructing a special swan raft on empty five-gallon oil drums. They anchored it in position and piled the beginning of a swan's nest on to it. The swans took it over and now every year they complete their nest, lay eggs, brood and hatch the cygnets; every time the tide comes in the nest and contents rise gently and float, serene and safe.

Family of blue tits at bird bath

Hen blackbird bathing. 'The object of the bath is to wet the plumage without actually soaking it'

A spotted flycatcher about to find a new use for some stray hair – birds are very willing to make use of cunningly provided nest material

A blackbird had built a nest and laid an egg underneath the wing of this car, though it had been in daily use

Blackbird's nest perched on a toolbag. Note that the female bird is a near-albino

Wren's nest in a coil of rope
◀

Marsh tit with food for nestlings. This nestbox would be a better one if the cracks between roof and walls were filled in – rain kills many nestlings
▼

In many villages in Germany, a cartwheel is fixed to the top of a high pole in the hope of attracting a stork to nest. And in Switzerland and Holland they have recently developed a successful pole-top nestbox for kestrels. If you have a large secluded garden in good kestrel country (and this includes some cities), you might consider the experiment of putting up one of these boxes worth trying. Farmers bothered with mice might also think it worth the effort. And it would be an interesting experiment to fix some to the giant electricity pylons that march through good kestrel country. These would provide excellent and safe fixing-posts (constructional details of the nestbox are given on page 35).

There are two basic types of nestbox: an enclosed space with small entrance hole, and a tray or ledge with or without sides and roof. They can be readily obtained at

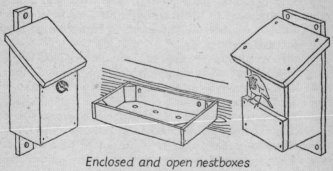

Enclosed and open nestboxes

reasonable prices (suppliers' addresses are given in Appendix B, page 101) or you may prefer to make your own; there is an extra satisfaction in seeing birds take over a nestbox you have built with your own hands. The method of construction will be discussed here in general terms, as the type of box and the critical sizes for each species will be found listed in the notes in Chapter 7. The nest-hole

T—B

measurement most people want to know straightaway is one
which excludes starlings and sparrows. The answer is
one-inch-and-an-eighth. But remember that blackbirds
and robins, for instance, live on the 'open plan' and need a
very large entrance opening. So make boxes of both types.

Although at first sight it may seem that the 'rustic' type
of nestbox will be most suitable I think the plain type is
preferable; the birds certainly do not seem to mind one
way or the other, so the main criteria are construction and
amenity. The plain square types are undoubtedly easiest
to make, and I think they look most attractive. The 'rustic'
boxes are usually made of birch. If they were only fixed to
birch trees I should have no objection, but this is seldom
the case. Birch boxes attached to oak or beech or elm trees
make rather an unhappy and unnatural contrast. Perhaps
there is some case for using rustic boxes when it is important
that they should not be too easily discovered, in public
places for instance, but I think it is a weak one. Small
boys on the warpath will discover either type in no time,
and if this is a danger the boxes should be fixed high, say,
not less than twelve feet.

The boxes should be made of three-quarter-inch wood,
which will stand up to weathering for a reasonable time
and be thick enough to insulate the interior temperature
from violent changes. Hardwood is most suitable as it is
more resistant to weather than softwood. Seasoned oak is
probably the best. Of the softwoods, cedar is quite satisfactory and weathers well. It is important that the box
should not warp and so allow wind and rain to attack the
nestlings. One side may be removable for cleaning purposes, but make sure that it fits firmly in position when in
use and that there is no danger of it falling out and exposing
the nest to predators. It is important that the roof fits flush
to the walls so that the box is as watertight as possible.
Seal the wall joints with a sealing compound, such as
Seelastik or Bostik, before you finally nail or screw the
pieces into position. Rain kills many nestlings in natural
nest sites and we should take particular care to exclude it

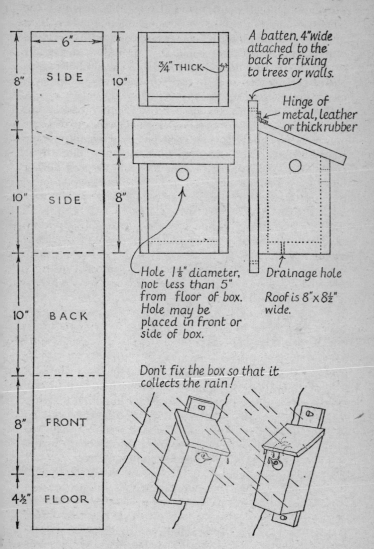

SIDE

6"

8"

10"

¾" THICK

10"

SIDE

10"

8"

BACK

Hole 1⅛" diameter, not less than 5" from floor of box. Hole may be placed in front or side of box.

8"

FRONT

4½"

FLOOR

A batten, 4" wide attached to the back for fixing to trees or walls.

Hinge of metal, leather or thick rubber

Drainage hole

Roof is 8" x 8½" wide.

Don't fix the box so that it collects the rain!

when we invite birds to use the boxes we provide. The
entrance hole should be at the top of the box, otherwise a
cat may be able to fish the young birds out, or they may be
seen by other predators when they stretch up to beg for
food. The inside floor measurements must allow birds
plenty of room to stretch their growing wings. Make a
ventilation hole in the floor.

Ideally, the nestboxes should be fixed in position in
October or November. This gives them a chance to weather
into their surroundings, and their potential occupiers have
plenty of time to get used to them and to explore their
possibilities. It may well be that they will be used during

the winter months as a roostbox. During the hard winter of
1961/62 there was one almost incredible case of a tit box
occupied by no less than fifty wrens, all huddling together
for warmth at night. Nestboxes may, of course, be put up
at any time in the winter, but if you are hoping they will
be occupied in their first spring, they ought to be up by the
end of February. However, better late than never.

The boxes can be fixed at about the six-foot level, though
the height is not the most important factor. The position
should be protected from prevailing cold winds and shaded
from the hot sun: as already mentioned, the box should
face somewhere in the arc from north through east to
south-east. The location should not be thickly sheltered or

darkened by foliage, and the adult birds must have a clear flight path to and from the nest. The entrance hole must be far enough from its fixing wall or tree-trunk to allow the incoming bird to have fully-stretched wings till the last moment before landing. Don't have a landing perch attached to the box, as this may provide a cat or a squirrel with a good position for extracting the babies. (If you want a perch for photographic purposes put it several feet away. The birds will probably be glad to use it as a staging-post.)

The box should be fixed in such a way that the top of the entrance hole wall is inclined outwards to exclude rain, and it should be secured to its anchorage by means of a batten, so that it does not become waterlogged where attached to the wall or trunk. It is important to fix the box firmly.

Do not put up too many boxes too close together. Like some of us, some birds prefer to keep their distance from each other (although this does not apply to colonial nesters like martins). Many species with a strong territorial instinct like to 'own' their plot but, fortunately, they do not as a rule object to members of other species living nearby. Thus robins, which have a highly-developed sense of territory, will not object to tits as close neighbours. It is difficult to say how many boxes should be erected because so many factors are involved, but where there is a large area to cover it is probably worth trying a dozen to the acre; more if the area is drastically short of natural nest sites. Put up twice as many enclosed boxes as open ones. If there are good natural or semi-natural sites available it may be that the boxes will be ignored altogether. On the other hand, blue tits may inspect, 'buy' and start building within a day of erection.

One more thing will help make your boxes attractive. Put a shallow layer of moss, or thin plaited straw, in the bottom of boxes destined for passerines. If you are hoping for a woodpecker, try priming the box with a sprinkling of sawdust or chippings and, as an appetizer, a few beetles and grubs. In early spring, when the birds are beginning to build, they will be searching everywhere for nesting materials. Jackdaws will take paper bags from litter-bins, or perch on a horse's back to steal hairs. When I was on the Galapagos Islands I once found a cormorant's nest that had a boat's rowlock ingeniously woven into the structure.

Birds are more than willing to be helped with their construction material problems. Straw, feathers, dog or cat combings, short bits of cotton, cotton wool, sheep wool and poultry down (after treatment with bug-powder) are all grist to their mill. Stuff them in two mesh bags – hanging one from the bird table or branch and pegging the other to the ground for ground-birds. There is nothing more charming than a sitting bird surrounded by a delicate garnish of coloured cottons. A naturalist once took a sparrow's nest to pieces and found it consisted of 1,282 separate items, which included 1,063 pieces of dead grass, 126 strips of bark, 15 pieces of paper, 10 pieces of cellophane, 13 pieces of tissue, 25 pieces of cotton thread, 28 wild bird feathers, one piece of string and a cotton bandage.

Woodpeckers or sparrows may 'improve' a nestbox, and in one case, a grey squirrel was reported to have enlarged a small hole to two and a half inches diameter. Do not worry too much about a nestbox that has had this treatment; a nuthatch may come along and plaster the edges of the hole to suit its own requirements. The RSPB make a metal plate, with a tit-size hole in it, which may solve the problem (see page 101).

If a starling should come and inspect your nestbox when you suspect another more welcome bird is considering it, there is a way of discouraging the unwanted guest. Fix a piece of rag or handkerchief to a long piece of string and arrange it so that you can joggle the rag from a concealed position indoors. The rag should be fairly close to the nest-box. When the starling comes near, operate the scaring device, but be careful not to disturb the bird you want to welcome. Never alter the position of a box after a bird has adopted it, and never disturb the bird while it is sitting. You will often hear people speak of the tameness of sitting birds; the truth is that the brooding instinct is stronger than the bird's terror of being close to a human. The privacy of a bird's nest should be respected and we should neither fuss nor photograph without good reason.

And when, at last, your nestbox contains a noisy, struggling muddle of baby birds, try to contain yourself and do not peer in too often. Examine the box every two or three days, and only when the adult bird is not at home. Nothing disconcerts a wild bird quite so much as the sudden appearance of a vast human face three inches away from it. Be particularly careful not to cause nearly-fledged birds to leave the nest too soon.

All birds are attacked by parasites such as fleas, lice and bird flies, so after the young have flown from the box it should be cleaned out and given a dose of bug-killer, e.g., Cooper's Poultry Aerosol. If you now prime the de-loused

box with a thin layer of moss it will, perhaps, serve for a second brood or be ready later on for use as a winter roostbox.

Finally, I must recommend an excellent and indispensable

field guide, *Nestboxes*, by Edwin Cohen, published by the British Trust for Ornithology, Beech Grove, Tring, Hertfordshire, and costing 3s. It is the definitive book on nestboxes and was written for research workers who use them for bird breeding studies.

4 *The bird table*

Having produced a garden full of food plants, nesting sites, drinking and bathing places, you could reasonably sit back and relax. Your birds are well cared for. But if you are prepared to go one step further, you can give yourself a great deal of extra pleasure. By providing food you can entice the birds to show themselves more freely in places where you can watch them. And, as the availability of food controls to some extent the bird population of your garden, you will also be increasing their numbers. But providing food is not a pleasure to undertake lightly. Put out some scraps in the garden and you will very soon attract new residents. They will become dependent on your generosity, and if it fails they will be competing for an inadequate supply of natural foods. Especially in cold weather birds may lose a lot of weight overnight, and they have to make it up again during the brief hours of daylight. Death comes in a matter of hours even to a healthy small bird, if it is without food. In hard weather the real killer is hunger, not cold.

The problems are simple enough to list: what to provide,

and how to serve it? You may think it sufficient simply to throw bread scraps on to the lawn, but this will not do at all. Bread alone, especially mass-produced white bread, is about as good for birds as it is for us, and certainly does not constitute a satisfactory diet. Besides, some birds do not care to come down to ground level for their food; in any case there is always the threat of a cat waiting in the wings! Again some birds are carnivorous and others vegetarian. It is no good offering a snail to a chaffinch, or a sunflower seed to a wren. A quick glance at a bird's bill will give a

clue to its diet. Finches have nutcracker bills, adapted to crack and crush, and they feed mostly on grain and seeds. They are hard-billed birds. In the other basic category, soft-bills, we have, for instance, robins and wrens with slender bills adapted to deal with grubs, caterpillars and other insects.

NATURAL FOOD

The best food to provide is what the birds would choose for themselves. One way to do this is to go on a nut and berry collecting expedition in the autumn. From August to October, you will be able to collect a fine harvest along the hedgerows. Pick the berries when they are just ripe.

In August your target should be the rowan. Later on, elderberries are first-quality bird food. Rowan and elder are probably the best berries, but wild cherry and haws are also good. Sloes do not seem to be very much liked by birds, nor are blackberries very popular either. Crab-apples are worth collecting, and in a bad winter you will find field-fares coming to the bird table for them. As for nuts, the best choice is the hazel, but almonds are also very useful, especially for pleasing great spotted woodpeckers. Collect conkers and sweet chestnuts, acorns and beech-mast from the ground as soon as they have fallen.

Dry the berries, and store both berries and nuts in a dry, dark place, and they will keep until you need them. Use shallow trays and arrange the fruits in a single layer. Gather pine and larch cones and take out the seeds from between the woody scales. Store all seeds, including weed-seeds such as thistle, knapweed, teazle, ragwort and stinging-nettle, in muslin bags, hung up where the air can get at them. In severe weather when the ground is hard with frost, take a spade and turn some earth over. This will provide a much-needed supplement to the bird-table food.

KITCHEN SCRAPS

Many people will tell you that birds love bread, and though this is true, nobody would suggest that bread alone provides a balanced diet. It is better than nothing and wholemeal is better than white, but it is a poor substitute for a varied selection of more nutritious food. Potato, especially baked in jacket, is a useful staple and much better than bread. Stale cake is good, especially if home-made with a high protein content. Minced raw meat, meat bones, cooked and chopped bacon-rinds and cheese are all good. An excellent use for fat is as a binding material for bird-pudding – the best kitchen-scrap bird offering of all, for which some recipes are given in Appendix A, page 99. Almost everything except highly-seasoned or salty food can go into the basket for bird kitchen-scraps. Don't worry

about giving birds something that may disagree with them; they will select what suits them and leave the rest. One way and another, you will not find much is wasted.

And, if you have one of those splendid whole Stilton cheeses at Christmas, don't throw away the near-empty shell when it is finished. Birds are very partial to Stilton, and prefer it when it is not swamped with port! Melon seeds can be another exotic bird-table success.

SPECIALLY-BOUGHT FOOD

There are several firms producing bird food (see list in Appendix A, page 100) and, if you can stand the expense, this is certainly an easy way to solve the supply problem. With 'Swoop', for instance, you have the advantage of knowing that the food is selected to satisfy a broad range of appetites. Incidentally, people occasionally find that some of the components of 'Swoop' are left uneaten on their bird table. This is simply because for one reason or another, their bird population has some missing links. Some species are confined to certain parts of the country, or there may be a local variation in their distribution. It is impossible to produce a bird food that will perfectly suit every locality, but you will not go far wrong with 'Swoop'.

Peanuts are, without a doubt, a 'best buy'. They are full of calories, convenient to handle, store and serve. Shelled, they cost about 6d a quarter in most stores. Unshelled, they can be strung up to serve as playthings for tits and nuthatches. Other nuts are all worth buying. Nuthatches, in particular, love brazils. Coconut is good, but serve it in

shell, not desiccated or ground, as this will swell up inside
a bird's stomach with dire results. Saw the nut in half and
hang it so that the rain cannot get in. I don't know whether
coconut juice is good for birds, but you might like to
experiment. Starlings love milk, and so do tits.

Mixed wild-bird seed can be bought from pet shops
at about 1s 6d a pound. But the most welcome seed, which
nuthatches love, is hemp. Split some for the smaller birds,
or buy it in crushed form. Sunflower, canary, millet, maize,
oats and corn are all good. Coarse oatmeal, costing about
9d a pound at chain-stores, should be offered raw, as
porridge is too glutinous and sticks to plumage and bill.
Rice, on the other hand, should be boiled before you serve
it.

You may be able to arrange with your local fruiterer
for a box of unsaleable fruit to be kept aside for you.
Apples, oranges, tomatoes, grapefruit, bananas and grapes
are all equally acceptable if you just cut them up. In hard
times, birds will eat this fruit ravenously, and in very cold
weather suet may usefully be added because it provides
energy so efficiently.

For live insect food, the best buys are mealworms and
ants' eggs. Robins are mad about mealworms. You can
buy them direct from petshops or bird-food suppliers, or
you can breed them yourself. (Addresses and do-it-yourself
directions are in Appendix A, page 99.) Serve the mealworms in a fairly deep, round dish, so that they cannot
escape – they are surprisingly mobile. Gentles are sometimes recommended, but, though I have not tasted them
myself, I think they are rather indigestible and a poor
substitute for mealworms. They are cheaper than mealworms, but nastier, and they should never be offered during
the breeding season, as they are quite unsuitable for nestlings. Ants' eggs (ant pupae) can be collected from under
stones in your garden; it is rather hard work for small
return but the birds will be grateful. And always put the
stone back in place so as not to upset the other creatures
whose roof it is. If you live near woods you may be able to

'Birds . . . have varying methods of hunting' (p. 47)

find the anthills of the wood ant. Dig into them and you will find masses of eggs that may be sieved and collected, though I always feel this is rather discourteous treatment of an inoffensive species.

Birds not only have varying food requirements, both in nature and at the bird table, but they also have varying methods of hunting. Some skulk about on the ground, some snoop along branches and foliage, and some run about on tree trunks and stone walls. So we must have variety of presentation as well as variety of food.

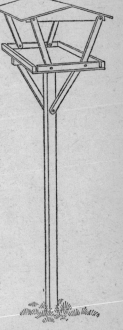

BIRD TABLES

The traditional way of feeding is with a bird table and, although it has limitations, it is on the whole a very satisfactory method. The table can either be supported on a post or it can hang from the bough of a tree, or a bracket. Your own situation will probably decide the method you use. There is little to choose between the two systems so long as you keep the cat problem firmly in mind and do not fix the hanging model to a potential cat-way. The feeding tray should not be too small. Somewhere between the two to four square feet mark is ideal. Put a coaming round the edge to stop the food being blown off, but leave a gap in it somewhere so that the table can be cleared and cleaned easily, and water can run off.

Whether it hangs or stands on a pedestal or post, the tray should be about five to six feet off the ground. The safest post is a piece of galvanized iron tubing, but any smooth pole will do. The worst support is one of those awful 'rustic' things that positively invite squirrels and cats to climb up to their burglarious work. The table should be in a position where it gets neither too much sun nor too much cold wind.

It should be within reasonable distance – say, a couple of yards – of cover, but out of cat-jumping range.

The tray does not need a roof but one is an advantage. A roof keeps the food drier, provides a place for a hanging seed-hopper, and may even be used as a roosting place at night. Birds will often use a covered bird table to shelter from a shower of rain. If the table has a roof-hopper, this should be kept full of mixed seed for the finches. On the tray, you can distribute your main offering of scraps and bird-pudding. Ideally, the food should be in pieces either so big that birds cannot carry it away, or so small that they do not want to carry it away: medium-sized bits tend to find their way to the nearest bush, where they get lost and encourage rats and mice. Another solution to this problem is to make a remo-vable, close-mesh, wire-netting frame which fits inside the coaming, covers the food, and prevents big birds flying off with large lumps.

A particularly fine type of bird table is used by my friend, E. H. Ware. He has rehabilitated the bottom part of a blown-down apple tree, cutting the trunk off just above the roots, and cutting the branches a couple of feet above the fork. With a tray fixed across the fork, and coconuts, feeders and suet-bag hanging from the ends of the branches, he has a good-looking and versatile feeding station. Another of its advantages is that it provides 'queuing space' for birds to wait their opportunity while a bully is monopolizing the tray.

SCRAP BASKETS

The advantage of scrap baskets is that the food is less likely to get blown about and scattered. The disadvantage is that thrushes and blackbirds cannot manage to hang on to them when they are suspended. The simplest scrap container is one of those netting bags that comes with a packet of carrots at the greengrocer's. However, it will soon get rather messy and, in the long run, it is best to buy a wire basket specially made for the job. The best one comes from the Royal Society for the Protection of Birds.

Scrap baskets made of collapsible wire mesh must be avoided as, with these, there is a danger that small birds may get a foot jammed between two moving pieces of wire. Sharp edges and potential leg-damagers must, in fact, be watched for on all feeding devices. Many small birds get leg injuries, and it may be that ill-made bird feeders are often to blame. One unusual hazard with small scrap baskets is that they may be stolen by crows. All the crow family are enthusiastic collectors, and I well remember a rook once stealing a bar of soap from my camp site. If you find your scrap basket being borrowed in this way, hang it under a tree where the thieves cannot see it and, after a day or two, return it to its normal hanging place.

SEED HOPPERS

The only practical way of providing seed is from a hopper. All other methods are very wasteful. (Even the hopper is susceptible to the aggressive methods of jays and great tits,

who scatter mixed seed while searching for titbits.) It is
important to keep the seed dry and the hopper must have a
good roof. The RSPB supply one which fits neatly into the
roof of their standard bird table. (See Appendix B, page
101 for more information.) If you have been on autumn
collecting expeditions, you will have a fine stock of your
own seeds; if not, any pet-shop will supply you with mixed
wild bird seed or canary seed. Keep the hopper well filled,
and do not risk a supply-failure in bad weather, because
the finches will have become dependent on your generosity.

NUTS

Peanuts are a bird's best friend, and the best way to present
them is to have a special wire-netting box, preferably with
a solid roof to keep the shelled nuts dry. (The Greenrigg
Works make an excellent grille peanut feeder.) You may
find yourself buying three pounds of nuts a week, but it will
be in a good cause. If you hang whole peanuts, do not use
multi-thread cotton or tits may get their legs trapped
between the strands. The best plan is to take a thin piece of
galvanized wire, about eighteen inches long, and cut it

obliquely at one end to make
a sharp point on which to
skewer the nuts. Bend the top
end into a hanging hook, and
the bottom end slightly up to
prevent the peanuts sliding
off. Attach the wire to its
anchor point by an elastic
band, and the whole thing
will twist around as birds
perch on it. Tits particularly

seem to enjoy twirling round in circles and are very amusing
to watch. The peanut skewer can hang from the bird table
or from a bough. Do not buy any of the feeders which are
made of spiral wire which terminates in a point at the lower
end. These are great leg-traps and should be avoided at all

costs. (See Appendix B for various nut-feeders which can be safely recommended.)

Some Americans recommend clamping a jar of peanut butter to a bird table, and though I have not tried this myself, it should be worth experiment. You can prevent any rain from getting in by fixing the jar at a slight down-hill angle. For other uses of nuts you might like to try jamming brazils into odd cracks and crannies in trees; nuthatches will appreciate this sort of treasure hunt. Any chestnuts you have collected in the autumn can be boiled and crushed for the tits. Hazel nuts, acorns and beech-mast should be served grated or finely chopped.

TIT-BELL

A tit-bell is the device H. Mortimer Batten made famous in the early days of Children's Hour on radio. Basically it is a very simple device. Fill a bell-mouthed or cup-shaped object with scraps and seed, then pour in hot fat. When the mixture has set, you hang the bell upside-down for the tits, nuthatches and woodpeckers to explore. Sparrows and starlings cannot get at the food, and it does not require too frequent replenishing. If you do not wish to buy the tit-bell you can make a perfectly good substitute from a half-coconut.

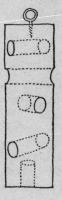

Another useful hanging device is the suet stick. For this, bore one-inch holes through a short length of birch log, stuff the holes with raw beef or kidney suet and hang it up. Woodpeckers are very fond of this gadget, but avoid fancy perches, or the starlings will take over.

GROUND FEEDING STATIONS

Many birds are reluctant to come to the bird table. Blackbirds and thrushes, dunnock and even moorhens will all come more easily to feed on the ground. The best plan is to put down a special tray for them, so that it can be taken in at night. Otherwise you will be encouraging rats. Do not put the tray too near a possible cat hiding-place, but see that it is within about six feet or so of cover. Just outside my office window, as I write, there are three dunnocks, a pair of yellow buntings, a chaffinch and a greenfinch all feeding happily on the ground below the bird table. Great tits get into the bird table seed-hopper and scatter the seeds as they search for bits of walnut, so that there are always easy pickings on the ground below. Many birds will hunt for crumbs under a bird table, and you may prefer to provide these ground-feeders with a nut-hopper of their own. If you are plagued with sparrows, a coarse wheat-hopper placed well away from your more expensive seed devices may keep them occupied.

WINDOW-SILLS

Even if you do not have a garden, you can still have a lot of fun providing a specialized bird-feeding station at your window-sill. You might devise a special adaptor for clamping the bird table to a sill, and most of the hanging devices can easily be suspended from a bracket. And even if you have a splendid garden, a window-sill feeding station is still desirable because, as sparrows and starlings are shy of it, you will be able to put out special delicacies for special birds. If possible, use a window-sill that is reasonably sheltered from both hot sun and cold winds. And, whatever feeding arrangements you may have, always remember that a constant supply of water is absolutely essential.

SELECTION PROBLEMS

Some people have a most unreasonable hatred of starlings. Personally, I find them beautiful and amusing to watch, although they can, occasionally, rather overwhelm one's facilities by sheer weight of numbers. By almost every post in the winter I get letters from people asking how they can make sure that other birds besides starlings get their fair share of the food. Sparrows, too, can be a nuisance as they tend to dominate other birds.

One way to cheat the starlings is to feed early or late. Starlings are late risers, and as they also flock away to roost early in the afternoon, you can cheat them with early morning and evening feeds for your garden residents. Another trick is to make a feeding cage of wire-mesh netting with an aperture too narrow for starlings to penetrate. If you put one-and-an-eighth-inch welded mesh netting round your bird table, it should keep the starlings out. The only disadvantage is that it also keeps thrushes and blackbirds out.

Starlings and sparrows tend to be shyer than other birds, so if you provide a feeding patch for them well away from your house and bird table, they may patronize it in preference to the 'home' feeding stations. This is where a window-sill comes into its own, providing tits, robins and finches with a reward for their tameness. I have already mentioned that a wheat-hopper may keep your sparrows busy while you feed tasty morsels to your favourites.

WHEN TO FEED

If you can feed at the same time every day, it is far and away the best method. Animals have built-in clocks and appreciate regularity. Early morning is best of all, as birds lose weight overnight and need a good start to the day. Obviously, the most important season for feeding is winter, when natural food supplies are scarce, and during a hard spell you may hold the lives of many small birds in your hands. So once again, I must emphasize that once you start feeding you must not stop. It is far better not to put out scraps at all if it is likely that, having started, you may later have to stop. The birds soon become dependent on your daily supplies, and if they are not forthcoming during cold weather when the ground is hard with frost, many of your pensioners may die. It is true that they have feathers which insulate them from the cold, but a body cannot function and keep warm without fuel.

When spring comes, the pattern of feeding should be altered. The amounts of heating foods such as suet and hemp should be reduced, and less bread should be given as this may fill a nestling bird with low-value bulk. Stale cake is better for nestlings, with live food for the insect-eaters. Search around for some snails and, at night, go out and collect slugs for your thrushes. Put out some meal-worms and ant pupae, if you wish, though this is the season when the birds are repaying you for your winter work. They will destroy hordes of insect pests far more safely than any chemical pesticide.

Keep feeding throughout the spring, summer and autumn, but with smaller quantities. This will keep your birds tame and, when you start increasing their supplies in late autumn, your happy band of pensioners will already know the ropes.

The feeding tray should not be too small - around three or four square feet is ideal. A coaming stops food blowing off.

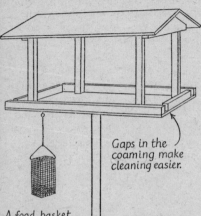

The R.S.P.B. table (above) is complete with chains for hanging and an adaptor for fitting to a post.

A food hopper is shown fitted under the roof.

Gaps in the coaming make cleaning easier.

A food basket for scraps or nuts is very popular with tits.

A galvanised tube or smooth pole is ideal.

About five or six feet high.

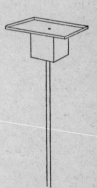

A biscuit tin fixed under the table is a useful anti-squirrel device.

5 *Predators and poisons*

A bird's life is fraught with natural hazards. After surviving a cold winter, it may get snapped up by a sparrowhawk. If it succeeds in finding a mate and hatching young, there may be a sudden shortage of food and the weaker nestlings may die. The chances of a wild bird living to a ripe old age are so remote as to be almost non-existent. So if we are going to invite birds to join us in our gardens there is an obligation on us to try to reduce the hazards.

Ideally, of course, you should completely seal your garden from unwelcome predators, but this is more easily said than done. Sparrowhawks are all part of the natural scene, but domestic cats and grey squirrels are most certainly not. There is no place for them in the bird garden, but you will never keep them out, short of total war. If you have a cat of your own, you may like to consider keeping it in for a reasonable and regular period each morning and before dusk, in order to give the birds time to feed. I have to admit that I like the company of a cat, and would not care to be without one, but the fact remains that Great Britain

is home to many millions of cats, every one of them super-
fluous to a good bird garden. You must make your own
decisions, but one thing is certain. You should not try to
tame your garden birds if you keep a cat. Feed them and
make homes for them by all means, but don't encourage
them to become too friendly or there will, inevitably, be a
tragic outcome.

If you can put up with it, a wire fence is undoubtedly
the best defence against other people's cats (and small
boys). This may seem a drastic and unsightly solution to
the problem, but it is surprising how, given some care in its
planning, a fence can be made to blend into its background.
One of the tricks is to use bitumen-dipped wire; this process
darkens the bright galvanized surface and makes it less
easy to see. Use heavy-gauge wire netting, six feet high,
with about eighteen inches sunk underground. At the top
of the wire there should be a T-piece overhang of eighteen
inches or so; at the bottom, the last four inches should be
bent at right-angles to the outside. Three-inch mesh is
standard, but the bottom section should be of one-inch mesh
to discourage rats. (For an excellent description of fence
erection, see *The Penguin Book of Pets* by Phil Drabble:
Penguin number PH 106).

If you don't want to go as far as installing a wire fence,
the best substitute is a thick and prickly hedge. Hawthorn
or holly hedges will both in time become fairly impenetrable, although you will always have to watch for secret
passageways and block them with bramble or thorn
cuttings. The disadvantage of a clipped hedge is that it will
not fruit very freely, though, on the other hand, it provides
good nesting sites. Allow some of the plants to mature so
that a few trees grow out of the hedge to blossom and fruit.
Holly is particularly good, because the dead leaves cover
the soil underneath with spiny points which may deter
cats, weasels, and such like.

Rats have to be taken seriously. They climb well, even
shinning up trees and hedges to search for eggs and young
birds, and a good bird garden is also an attractive rat

garden. So food should not be left on the ground at night, and windfalls too should be cleared away every evening: they can become part of the winter bird-table menu.

The best way to deal with rats is to use a safe poison, or to put plenty of traps under cover in the dark places they like. Place a five- or six-foot drainpipe (six-inch section) in the likely places, and put a killer food bait – 'Warfarin' is probably the safest – in the middle of it. Mechanical rat-traps are only moderately successful. Rats are suspicious creatures and if you try traps put one each side of a bait placed in the middle of the pipe-length. Cheese, apple, cake, almost anything will do as bait. Set the traps before dusk and examine them when it is dark. Don't leave them set up all night or you might trap a cat.

Grey squirrels, too, are unwelcome visitors to the bird garden. They may appear charmingly acrobatic as they leap from branch to branch, but they are great egg-eaters. They will even enlarge the hole of a nestbox to lift out the nestlings. Grey squirrels are an introduced species which have become a considerable hazard, and should be severely controlled. You must harden your heart and shoot or trap them. You should also discourage jays and magpies, for there is no doubt that they will take any small birds' eggs and young they can find. On the other hand, they are both handsome birds and have a welcome place in the natural scene.

The greatest bird menace of all, however, is the residual organo-chlorine insect-icide. After years of trial and a growing weight of evidence against them, it is depressing to find that farmers still use dangerous seed-dressings and sprays, and that garden shops still sell harmful and extravagant garden 'aids'. If you have the least feeling for wild life and, incidentally, if you value your own health, you should refuse to use organo-chlorine pesticides and you should encourage others to do the same. Our environment is becoming increasingly polluted with chemicals whose long-term effects are unknown but highly suspect. Many of the pesticides sold freely in shops are dangerous, not only to the pests they set out to destroy but to useful animals, as well as, ultimately, to ourselves. The insects killed or half-killed by such substances are eaten by birds, and the poison the insect contained is not completely excreted by the bird but stored up in its fat. So it follows that a not very toxic chemical, such as Rhothane or DDT, may, if persistent, be hazardous. Other birds and mammals feed on these birds and obtain a much larger dose, which they in turn accumulate. In other words, these dangerous substances are liable to build up in birds and animals at the end of the food chain. Poisoning of this kind may not only kill, but may apparently affect fertility.

This is not to suggest that we stop waging war against pests, but it is worth pointing out that sprays do dangerously just that which birds do safely. Finches, tits, tree-creepers and wrens all patrol and police leafy places and decimate the caterpillar and insect population. Thrushes (and hedgehogs) help with your snails and slugs. En-courage the birds, save yourself money, and give yourself pleasure at the same time. It is true that birds will also eat some of your soft fruit and spoil some of the buds of your fruit trees, but this is a small price to pay for the pleasure they will give and for the knowledge that yours is a poison-free garden. On balance, birds do more good than harm.

The Ministry of Agriculture, Fisheries and Food has recommended that home gardeners should *not* use the following pesticides: Aldrin; Dieldrin; Endrin; Endosulfan; and Rhothane. Note that these are not, necessarily, the brand names displayed in large type on the label. One must read the small type on the tin or packet to discover whether the preparation is dangerous or not.

DDT, BHC, lindane and chlordane, are also persistent organo-chlorine insecticides. No ban has yet been put on these chemicals but tighter government control seems inevitable. Meanwhile, the Ministry of Agriculture recommends that DDT and BHC, including lindane, should be used *with restraint* by gardeners. Be careful with half-empty and even empty containers, dispose of them in such a way that their contents cannot contaminate soil or water. Any chemical should be used sparingly, with care and exactly according to the directions on the label; ideally it should not be used at all.

Some insecticides appear to be reasonably safe. Pyrethrum and derris, for example, are potent insect-killers which are not harmful to warm-blooded creatures. They do not accumulate, to be passed on through the food chain. Nicotine and malathion also do not accumulate but are more poisonous and require great caution in handling. Derris is dangerous to fish, so do not use it if there is any likelihood of it finding its way into a pond or stream.

Pyrethrins are extracted from a white-flowered crop grown in the highlands of Kenya, and are the basis of a number of safe pesticides. As insects do not build up resistance to pyrethrum it is more efficient in the long run, although it may not have quite the sensational and immediate effect of some of the dangerous organo-chlorine preparations. But use the spray in the evening, to spare the bees. Pyrethrum will control most flying and crawling insect pests such as ants, blackfly, caterpillars, flea beetles, greenfly, sawfly, whitefly and thrips.

Finally, to save yourself needless expense and to develop a healthy poison-free garden, get a copy of a most excellent and invaluable booklet *Pest Control Without Poisons*, by Lawrence D. Hills, published by the Henry Doubleday Research Association, Bocking, Braintree, Essex, and costing 3s. This association is now experimenting with the possibilities of controlling insect pests by luring them to a trap by means of scents. (See their report *Perfumes Against Pests*, 3s 6d.)

6 *Why only birds?*

Birds tend to get more than their fair share of attention. Other animals are equally interesting and entertaining, and often equally beneficial to the garden. Take insects, for instance. Most people regard all insects as pests whereas, in fact, only a few hundred out of more than 20,000 British species can reasonably be classified as harmful; by harmful, I mean those that interfere with man's activities, damage crops and so forth. No doubt, the pests themselves would take a different view, and many of the species not only live without encroaching on our lives, but are of great benefit to us. Pollinating bees are an obvious example of how useful insects can be, and a wide variety of flies, beetles, butterflies, moths and wasps also pollinate many flowers. Ladybirds, too, are useful, preying on such harmful insects as aphids and thrips, so if you find a winter colony hibernating in some crevice, leave them in peace. Dragonflies are also useful, eating many other insect species which we regard as harmful. Above all, spiders are useful, eating a great quantity of insects.

Toads are interesting creatures to attract to your garden.

Provide a convenient home for one – a hole in a wall, a cavity under a stone or plank – and it may stay with you for years and become a family pet. One naturalist had a toad living under his doorstep for thirty-six years. Toads have a well-developed memory for locality, and though they may forage long distances for food, they will return safely afterwards. They will come out in the daytime in a heavy shower but, normally, they feed in the late evening and early at night. They eat snails, beetles, ants and other insects, caterpillars, woodlice and worms, and will even take snakes and mice.

Although some of the small mammals are unwelcome visitors, there is one shining exception – the hedgehog. Hedgehogs make charming friends and no garden should be without one, although I would never suggest keeping one in captivity. Unless your garden is very large, your hedgehog will want to wander a great deal, but if you provide the right facilities it may use your premises as its base. To my mind, this is the most rewarding of all animal relationships. With a captive animal you can never be quite certain that it is content. A free-living, wild creature which chooses to settle with you will give much deeper pleasure, and provide a never-ending source of interest.

Quite apart from their engaging habits, hedgehogs are positively useful. They eat formidable quantities of slugs, millipedes and caterpillars, but not useful insects such as ladybirds, devil's-coach-horse and violet ground-beetles. They even eat adders, on occasion, though I would not classify the adder as a pest.

Hedgehogs can be attracted in much the same way as birds. Food must be put out for them and they must be provided with nestboxes. They are nocturnal creatures, coming out to feed at dusk from late March to November. (In the winter they hibernate.) Put out a saucer of milk, and if it has been turned upside down by the morning you can be reasonably sure that a hedgehog has been at it. (Believing it to be a log, they turn it up to see if there are any tasty insects underneath.) They need to have water, too, but

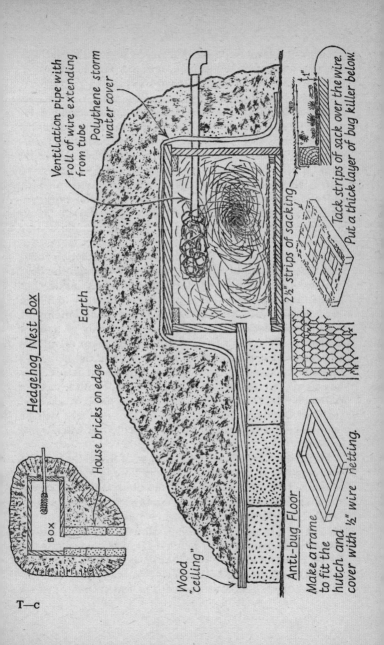

Hedgehog Nest Box

Ventilation pipe with roll of wire extending from tube

Polythene storm water cover

Earth

House bricks on edge

BOX

Wood "ceiling"

2½" strips of sacking

Tack strips of sack over the wire. Put a thick layer of bug killer below.

Anti-bug Floor

Make a frame to fit the hutch and cover with ½" wire netting.

T—c

your ground-level bird bath will serve very well. Hedgehogs are also fond of tinned salmon, oranges, and tomatoes, as well as the more obvious kitchen scraps.

A most interesting design for a hedgehog nestbox has been developed by the Henry Doubleday Research Association (see Hedgehogs and the Gardener, at the end of this chapter) and, with permission, I am reproducing the dimensions and details of their hog-kennels. The box should be about 12 in. by 15 in. by about 13 in. high, and made of untreated timber. (Hedgehogs have a keen sense of smell, objecting to both tobacco smoke and artificial preservatives.) To prevent cats getting in, there should be an entrance tunnel a couple of feet long and with a $4\frac{1}{2}$-in. square section.

It is important that there should be a ventilation shaft, and that air should be able to pass freely through the box; otherwise it will become uncomfortably wet inside. But bear in mind that the hedgehog will probably try to fill the box very full with hay and make sure the ventilation pipe doesn't get blocked. Perhaps the best plan is to make a simple 'baffle' with a fairly tightly rolled piece of chicken wire (see illustration). Fit it firmly so that the hedgehog doesn't dislodge it while he's thrashing about inside. The box needs to be rainproof so cover the roof with a piece of polythene that just overlaps the sides of the box. (Do not seal the box completely with polythene or there will be condensation troubles and the inside of the box will become sodden.)

Hedgehogs are liberally infested with fleas and ticks, so you may like to provide an anti-bug floor. This is a luxury of course! Make it as shown in the illustration and spread the floor underneath with a safe insecticide. (Try 'Herbalsectide', a derris and pyrethrum mixture made up by Kathleen Hunter, Barcaldine House, Connel, Argyll, Scotland. It costs 4s 6d for four ounces, post paid. But please be very careful to make sure that none of it gets into ponds or aquaria for it will kill fish.)

Cover the whole assembly with at least a foot of earth,

so that just the entrance tunnel and feeding hatch are visible. Hedgehogs like to have plenty of dry bedding in their homes, so make some hay or dry leaves available near the box entrance. Put it in a container so that it doesn't get wet and they'll drag it across to the box entrance, leaving some odd bits on the way as evidence.

If there are any hedgehogs in your locality (dead bodies on the road are a certain clue), one will soon discover and adopt your box. Otherwise, you may choose to import one. It is no bad thing to collect hedgehogs found in the road, because they are in danger from passing traffic and you are doing them a good turn by rescuing them. However, this should only be done at times when it is unlikely that you are rescuing a female hedgehog which has a nest of babies somewhere. Unfortunately, there is no easy way of sexing hedgehogs. You are safe enough in taking young ones – up to Spanish orange size – at any time, but adults should only be collected in early spring until mid-May, in August, and again from mid-October. Powder the hedgehog with bug-killer to rid it of its parasites before you release it in your garden. Hedgehogs usually have two litters a year; the gestation period is somewhere between thirty-one and forty days, and the lactation period about four weeks. The young are born blind, their eyes are open at fourteen days and, when three weeks old, they leave the nest, following mother in Indian file.

With luck your box will be occupied all the year, although hedgehogs won't necessarily raise families in it. During the spring and summer an individual may simply use it as a bedroom during the day. But of course he may well choose to hibernate in it when the time comes. Feed your hogs well in autumn, so that they face the long sleep with good reserves of fat. They may be fairly inactive in October if the weather is cold, but true hibernation starts much later and probably in December. Even after this the hedgehog may well make occasional sallies into the great outdoors. They usually emerge from hibernation in March.

You will soon get to know when the hedgehog comes out to feed and, if you provide a feeding station nearby, you will find that the animal is very tame and will take titbits, especially mealworms, from your hand. Avoid sudden noises, move and talk quietly.

One last warning. If you encourage hedgehogs, or any other animal for that matter, to live in your garden – do not use organo-chlorine garden pesticides of any kind.

Read: *Beneficial Insects*, by B. D. Moreton: Bulletin No. 20 of the Min. of Ag. and Fish: published by HM Stationery Office. 3s 6d.

Hedgehogs and the Gardener: published by the Henry Doubleday Research Association, Bocking, Braintree, Essex. 2s 6d.

7 Species notes – birds which use nestboxes or visit feeding stations

There are no identification notes in the following list, which is arranged in the Wetmore order of classification. Probably the best reference book for straightforward bird identification is *A Field Guide to the Birds of Britain and Europe*, by Peterson, Mountfort and Hollom, published by Collins. For identification notes plus detailed information on habitat, distribution, behaviour, food and breeding (in the wild) the most useful single volume is *The Popular Handbook of British Birds*, by P. A. D. Hollom, published by H. F. and G. Witherby. Further information on nestboxes can be found in the three-shilling pamphlet *Nestboxes*, by E. Cohen, published by the BTO, Beech Grove, Tring, Herts.

Additions and corrections to the food preference and nestbox sections in the following notes will be welcomed.

MALLARD (Wild Duck). *Anas platyrhynchos*. Resident and generally distributed. Fresh water, sea coast and estuary.

Feeds on seeds, buds, leaves of land and water plants, insects and other small water animals. Will come to suitable feeding stations in shallow water for corn or to water's edge for scraps, although this will depend on the degree of tameness achieved. (Many wild mallard join semi-domesticated duck collections.)

Nests in thick undergrowth not far from water. Sometimes in pollard willows, tree holes, second-hand crow-type nests, etc. Grass, leaves, rushes, feathers, down. Lays about a dozen eggs, greyish-green or greenish-buff, occasionally clear pale blue, February onwards. Incubation, four weeks; fledging, seven and a half weeks. One or two broods.

Nestbox: Try providing an apple box or large, open cat basket in typical nest site. Where mallards have become very tame (in village ponds and the like) try erecting an open-ended barrel on an island.

Read: *Wildfowl in Great Britain*, edited by G. Atkinson-Willes, Nature Conservancy Monograph No. 3, HMSO, 1965.

CANADA GOOSE. *Branta canadensis.* Resident and widely distributed. An introduced species. Grassland and marshes near lakes, meres.

Grazes in flocks on grassland. Also takes water plants. Will come to hand-feed on corn or bread when tame.

Nests on islands and marshes, sheltered by undergrowth or bush. Nest-hollow lined with grasses, leaves, reeds, down and feathers. Five or six white eggs. Late March/April. Incubation, four weeks; fledging, six weeks. One brood.

Nestbox: Box or platform raised on posts above water-level or on raft. Make an artificial island, plant clumps of iris, reeds, sedge, etc., to provide artificial nest-site. *Warning!* Canada Geese (gander especially) can be very aggressive in the breeding season, and have been known to attack human beings, even wounding children.

MUTE SWAN. *Cygnus olor.* Generally distributed. Open water, ponds, parks, sheltered sea coasts and lochs.

Dips head and neck, or 'up-ends' to graze on underwater vegetation; also takes roots and buds of aquatic plants, small frogs, tadpoles, fish. Will come to hand or feeding station for scraps.

Nests almost anywhere near water, in a large heap of vegetation. Five to seven eggs, almost white, tinged with greyish or bluish green. April/May. Incubation, about thirty-five days; fledging, about four and a half months. One brood. *Warning!* Aggressive at nest.

Nestbox: Artificial island or raft, primed with a pile of vegetation.

Read: *The Royal Birds*, Lillian Grace Paca, St Martin's Press, New York, 1963.

KESTREL. *Falco tinnunculus.* Resident, generally distributed, except in winter in far north. At present decreasing in numbers. Moors, coast, farmland and open woodland.

Perches on trees, posts, wires or buildings, watching out for its prey. Hunts in the open, checking frequently to hover in characteristic attitude, watching for beetles or small mammals.

Makes no nest, but lays eggs in a scrape on cliff ledge or in second-hand crow or magpie nest. Sometimes in tree hollow or ledge on building or ruin. About five eggs, the white ground colour often hidden by red-brown splotchings. Mid-April onwards. Incubation twenty-eight days; fledging, twenty-eight days. One brood.

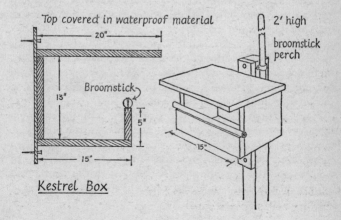

Kestrel Box

Nestbox: Open-fronted type, 25 by 15 by 15 inches high, with roof overhanging a couple of inches. One of the long sides is partly open, having only a five-inch high board along the bottom part, fitted with a broom-pole size lip to enable the bird to perch easily before entering. Fix a two-foot broomstick vertically on top as a perch. Prime the box with some peat mould. Fix on eighteen- to thirty-foot pole, or high on side of house, where some shelter is available from midday sun. Hope a jackdaw doesn't find it first.

PHEASANT. *Phasianus colchicus.* Resident and generally distributed except in Ireland. Much-preserved as a game bird. Woodland edge, cultivated land, parkland, large secluded gardens and shrubberies, damp, rushy and sedgy fields.

Forages on ground for varied selection of animal and vegetable food. Fruit, seeds, grain, insects, worms, slugs. Will come to secluded garden ground station for corn.

Nests under cover of ferns, brambles, etc., in woods, copses, hedgerows and reed-beds, making a hollow in the ground and lining it with a few stems of grass and dead leaves. Eight to fifteen olive-brown eggs. Early April onwards. Incubation, twenty-two to twenty-seven days; fledging, twelve to fourteen days. One brood.

MOORHEN (Waterhen). *Gallinula chloropus.* Resident and widely distributed. Fresh-water ponds, slow streams, marshes and water-meadows.

Forages on grassland and waterside vegetation. Food is mostly vegetable, but includes a fair proportion of animals, such as worms, slugs, and snails. Will soon get used to coming to scraps on the ground; flies less readily up on to the bird table. Watch out for rats.

Nests among waterside plants or trees, building an open structure of reeds, flags, sedge, etc. Five to eleven eggs, whitish-grey to buff or greenish with suffused red-brown spots. End of March onwards. Incubation nineteen to twenty-two days; fledging period: in nest two or three days if undisturbed, then another three to five weeks with family. Generally two broods.

Read: *A Waterhen's Worlds*, by H. Eliot Howard, Cambridge University Press, 1940.

TURNSTONE. *Arenaria interpres.* Winter visitor to rocky or pebbly coasts, although many non-breeders stay for the summer.

Roots about in small parties over rocks or shore, searching for small seashore animals in weed and tide-line debris. Came eagerly to regular beach feeding station for bread, cake, peanuts and scraps in South Devon, and I suggest others should try the experiment. (Winwood Reade tells me that turnstones also come to feed outside the army camp kitchen on the remote island of St Kilda.)

Breeds from Arctic Circle to points north.

HERRING GULL. *Larus argentatus.* Resident, generally distributed along coasts, estuaries, waters and fields often far inland.

Opportunist feeder, eating almost anything, but mostly animal food. Will come to bird table or ground station for almost anything, but is shy and not particularly welcomed by other birds.

Nests in colonies on cliff ledges, grassy coastal slopes, sand dunes and shingle. Large nest of grass or sea-weed. About three eggs, olive to umber, sometimes pale blue or green, splotched with deep blackish-brown. End April to early June. Incubation, twenty-six days; fledging, six weeks. One brood. Of recent years it has taken to nesting on cottage roofs and chimney pot areas in West Country fishing villages where fish scraps are freely available. Not to be encouraged, though, as it can be aggressive in defence of its young.

Read: *The Herring Gull's World*, Niko Tinbergen, Collins, 1953.

BLACK-HEADED GULL. *Larus ridibundus.* Resident and widely distributed. Coastal and inland species frequenting lakes, sewage-farms, harbours and farmland.

Feeds around low-lying shores and estuaries, freely inland to farms, lakes and rivers. Food very varied, animal and vegetable. Will come fairly freely to bird feeding stations in open situations.

Nests in colonies among sandhills, sandbanks, lake islands and shingle. Rough nest of vegetable matter. About three eggs, light buffish-stone to deep umber brown, splotched dark blackish-brown. Mid-April onwards. Incubation, twenty-two to twenty-four days; fledging, six weeks. One brood.

STOCK DOVE. *Columba oenas.* Resident and well distributed, except in northern Scotland. Open parkland, wooded country, cliffs and sand dunes.

Feeds over fields and open ground, taking vegetable leaves, beans, peas and grain.

Nests in holes in old trees, rocks, rabbit-burrows, buildings. Unsubstantial structure of few twigs, bits of grass, or nothing at all. Two creamy-white eggs. End March till July. Incubation, sixteen to eighteen days; fledging, twenty-eight days. Two, sometimes even three, broods.

Nestbox: Enclosed. 8 in. diameter entrance hole, 15 in. interior depth, 15 in. by 25 in. floor. Or alternatively, box similar to that for kestrel, but mounted on tree.

ROCK DOVE. *Columba livia.* Resident, but decreasing in numbers and hopelessly inter-bred with its own descendant, the domestic pigeon. The only pure rock doves that remain are probably to be found on the north and west coasts of Scotland and Ireland. Rocky sea-cliffs and coastal fields.

Forages on coastal pastureland for grain, peas, beans, potatoes, seeds, etc.

Nests in sea-caves or among rocks in wilder parts of coast. Few bits of heather or roots in a hole or cave-ledge or crevice. Two white eggs, April onwards. Incubation, seventeen to nineteen days; fledging, four or five weeks. Two or three broods.

Rock doves were domesticated hundreds of years ago in Scotland. Artificial nesting ledges were provided for them in convenient sea-caves, and the resulting squabs farmed for food. The flourishing domestic forms of the rock dove (feral pigeons) have confused the wild status of the bird in no uncertain fashion. The feral pigeon breeds freely in cities and places where it can take advantage of man's soft heart and kitchen scraps.

WOOD PIGEON (Ring Dove). *Columba palumbus.* Resident and generally distributed except in extreme north of Scotland. Open country of all kinds, provided there are some trees.

Feeds mainly on ground, but in spring will graze over foliage, buds and flowers in trees. Main food vegetable, cereals, roots, beans, peas and seeds. Will come to garden feeding station for ground food, bread, vegetable scraps, seeds, and may even visit the bird table. A partiality to beans and peas may make it unwelcome.

Nests in tall hedgerows, almost any kind of tree, second-hand crow nests and squirrel dreys. Sometimes on ground or on building ledges in towns, where it has overcome shyness. Few twigs (you can often see the outline of the eggs if you stand under the flimsy nest). Normally two white eggs. April to September. Incubation, seventeen days; fledging, about three weeks. Three broods usually.

Read: *The Wood Pigeon,* R. K. Murton, Collins, 1965.

COLLARED DOVE. *Streptopelia decaocto.* Resident and widely distributed. Vicinity of farm-buildings, park-like places and gardens in towns and villages.

Finds its food in close relationship with man, sharing grain with chickens, raiding corn and stack-yards. In parks and gardens will also take berries and young foliage. Comes freely to bird table and ground feeding station for seeds, peas, grain and scraps.

Nests in trees, preferably conifers, on a flimsy platform of sticks, grasses and roots. Two white eggs. March to October. Several broods.

Ten years ago this species did not figure on the British List, yet it is now found throughout the country, the result of a remarkable cross-Europe invasion originating from India.

BARN OWL. *Tyto alba.* Resident, generally distributed, but not abundant. Vicinity of farms, old buildings, church towers, etc. Parkland with old timber.

Hunts over fields and open country for small rodents and even small birds.

Nests in ruins or unoccupied buildings, hollow trees and cliff crevices. No material used, the eggs are often surrounded by a pile of castings. Four to seven white eggs. April to July. Incubation, thirty-two to thirty-four days; fledging, about ten weeks. Frequently two broods.

Nestbox: Open tray 36 in. long, 15 in. wide and 12 in. deep. Divide interior into two equal areas with a cross-wise partition 7 in. or 8 in. deep. An apple box would probably serve the purpose, with the top 6 in. of the middle partition knocked out. The tray should be placed just inside and below a large (one or two feet diameter) entrance hole to a suitable building, loft or large recess well above the ground. The owls will nest in the section of the tray further from the hole.

LITTLE OWL. *Athene noctua.* An introduced species, now resident in the southern half of England. Open farmland.

Hunts mainly at dusk and early morning for small mammals, insects and a few birds.

Nests in trees, farm-building holes and rabbit burrows. Three to five white eggs. April, May. Incubation, twenty-eight to twenty-nine days; fledging, about twenty-six days. Usually one brood.

Nestbox: Enclosed type, at least 4 in. diameter hole, inside depth 12 in., floor $7\frac{1}{2}$ in. square. Also open type similar to kestrel box.

TAWNY OWL. *Strix aluco.* Resident and generally distributed in Great Britain, but never recorded wild in Ireland. Woodland, farmland, parks and well-timbered gardens.

Hunts at dusk for small mammals, birds and insects, even frogs and newts.

Nests in tree holes, second-hand crow, hawk and heron nests, squirrel dreys. Sometimes in barns and rock ledges. Two to four white eggs. Late March, early April. Incubation, twenty-eight to thirty days; fledging, about four weeks. One brood.

Nestbox: Enclosed type, 8 in. diameter hole at top, inside depth 30 in., floor 8 in. square. (An alternative chimney type is described in the BTO Field Guide *Nestboxes*.) Will also use a nine-gallon cider barrel if a hole is opened in it and the barrel put in a tree crotch about 12 ft. high.

SWIFT. *Apus apus.* Summer resident, generally distributed except in north-west Scotland, arriving late April, early May, leaving early August. Habitat exclusively aerial. Very rarely seen at rest except on the nest.

Feeds on the wing, taking only insects, anywhere from ground level to 1,000 feet.

Nests in colonies, under eaves, in crevices and in holes. Bits of straw, grass, feathers, seed fluff, collected on the wing and stuck together with saliva to form a cup. Two or three white eggs. Late May, early June. Incubation, eighteen to nineteen days; fledging, about six weeks. One brood.

Nestbox: Complicated design, see BTO Field Guide. Or open out a narrow slit in eaves to allow entrance to roof.

Read: *Swifts in a Tower*, David Lack, Methuen, 1956.

KINGFISHER. *Alcedo atthis.* Resident and generally distributed, but scarce and decreasing. Streams, rivers, canals, lakes.

Perches or hovers above water, fish-watching. Plunges to capture small fish, insects, larvae and amphibians. In winter, visits coast for shrimps, prawns, small rock-pool fish, etc. May come to garden ponds for minnows or sticklebacks.

Nests in tunnels in banks of streams or sand-pits. Six to seven white eggs. Late April to August. Incubation, nineteen to twenty-one days; fledging, twenty-three to twenty-seven days. Two broods.

HOOPOE. *Upupa epops.* Passage-migrant, regular in small numbers in spring, less frequent in autumn, on south, south-east and south-west coasts, and on east coast as far north as Norfolk. Elsewhere rare in Great Britain. Open woodland, orchards, parkland.

Feeds mainly on ground, often close to human habitation, probing on lawns for insect larvae, etc. Does not often come to bird station, but might do so if mealworms /caterpillars / ant pupae were made available in dish. Not shy.

Normally breeds in Eurasia, but occasionally a hoopoe will nest in one of the southern coastal counties, choosing tree holes, crevices and holes in rough stone walls and ruins. Five to eight eggs, whitish-grey or yellowish-olive. May / June. Incubation, eighteen days; fledging, twenty to twenty-seven days. Two broods.

Nestbox: Uses them in Europe and, presumably, may do so here.

GREEN WOODPECKER. *Picus viridis*. Resident, but local in England and Wales, rare in Scotland, none in Ireland. Deciduous woods, park and farmland.

Searches for insect larvae over tree trunks and branches, probing with long mobile tongue; also feeds freely on ground, especially where there are ant's nests. In times of hard frost, when ant hills are frozen solid, it may damage beehives by boring holes to reach the insects within. May also attack nestboxes. Will visit bird table for mealworms, bird pudding, etc.

Nests in tree trunks, boring a hole horizontally two or three inches, then descending to make a nest compartment over a foot deep and about six inches wide at its broadest. A few chips at the bottom form the nest. Sometimes, old holes are used again. Five to seven translucent eggs. End April to May. Incubation, eighteen to nineteen days; fledging, eighteen to twenty-one days. One brood.

Nestbox: Enclosed type, with 2½ in. entrance hole, 15 in. interior depth, 5 in. square floor. Ideal for starlings!

Read: *My Year with the Woodpeckers*, Heinz Sielmann, Barrie & Rockliff, 1959.

GREAT SPOTTED WOODPECKER. *Dendrocopus major.* Resident, widely distributed in England, central and southern Scotland, none in Ireland. Wooded country – coniferous in north, deciduous in south – hedgerows, orchards and large gardens.

Hunts over trees for insect larvae, spiders, seeds and nuts, even wedging a nut into a tree crack to deal with it. Will come to bird table for suet especially; also oats, nuts, boiled fat bacon, hanging fat, or nuts. As adept as tits at feeding upside down.

Nests in tree holes ten feet and higher from ground. Few wood chips form nest. Four to seven white eggs. May to June. Incubation, sixteen days; fledging, eighteen to twenty-one days. One brood.

Nestbox: Enclosed type, entrance hole 2 in., interior depth 12 in., floor 5 in. square. Also ideal for starlings.

Read: *My Year with the Woodpeckers*, Heinz Sielmann, Barrie & Rockliff, 1959.

LESSER SPOTTED WOODPECKER. *Dendrocopus minor.* Resident in southern England and midlands, becoming local and rarer further north. Widely distributed but scattered in Wales. Not in Scotland or Ireland. Same type of country as greater spotted.

Elusive bird, searching upper parts of trees for insect larvae. Will come somewhat nervously and rarely to bird table for fats, nuts and fruit.

Bores nest-hole in decayed soft wood of branch or tree trunk. A few chips make nest. Four to six translucent eggs, early May to mid-June. Incubation, fourteen days; fledging, twenty-one days. One brood.

Read: *My Year with the Woodpeckers*, Heinz Sielmann, Barrie & Rockliff, 1959.

WRYNECK. *Jynx torquilla.* Summer resident. Decreasing and scarce, possibly as few as one hundred breeding pairs, mostly in East Anglia. Open parkland, heaths, hedgerows, sometimes orchards, gardens.

Picks up insects from tree surface, clinging to trunk like woodpecker. Sometimes on ground, picking up ants, insect larvae. Feeds occasionally at bird tables.

Nests in natural or improved tree or bank holes. No nesting material. Seven to ten white eggs. End May till July. Incubation, twelve days; fledging, nineteen to twenty-one days. Usually one brood.

Nestbox: Enclosed, with 1⅜ in. by 1¼ in. diameter entrance, 6 in. interior depth, 5 in. square floor.

SWALLOW. *Hirundo rustica.* Summer resident. Generally distributed. Open farmland, meadows, ponds. Spends much time in flight, especially over water, hunting insects from ground level to 500 feet. Unlike swift, settles freely on buildings and wires. Seldom on ground, except when collecting mud for nest.

Nests on rafters and joists, building open mud and straw cup, lined with grasses and feathers. Four to five eggs, white spotted with red-brown. Mid-May till October. Incubation, fifteen days; fledging, three weeks. Usually two broods.

Nestbox: Improvise a simple saucer-shape, or fix a half-coconut or 4 in. by 4 in. shallow wooden tray to joist or rafter, even as low as six feet. Will also use specially adapted house-martin nest (q.v.).

HOUSE MARTIN. *Delichon urbica.* Summer resident, generally distributed. Habitat as swallow, but more often near human habitation.

Hunts insects on the wing, especially over water. Also on the ground.

Originally a cliff-nester, but has adapted itself to buildings. Nests in colonies on outside walls of buildings, under eaves. Cup shape made of mud and lined with straw and feathers. Four to five white eggs. Late May to October. Incubation fourteen to fifteen days; fledging, nineteen to twenty-one days. Usually two broods.

Nestbox: Special artificial nest obtainable from supplier listed in Appendix B (Clent House Gardens). Fix under eaves or window-sill. For best results an existing house martin colony should be close at hand. One nest may suffice, but the more the merrier.

SAND MARTIN. *Riparia riparia.* Summer resident, widely distributed. Open country with water.

Feeds mainly over water, taking insects on the wing. Perches on wires and low branches, and will occasionally pick insects from the ground while on the wing.

Nests in colonies, making a long hole with a nest chamber at the end, in sand and gravel pits, railway cuttings, river banks and sea cliffs. Few straws and feathers form nest. Four to five white eggs. Mid-May onwards. Incubation, fourteen days; fledging, nineteen days. Two broods.

Nestbox: Specially devised tunnel-box (see BTO guide, *Nestboxes*). Or try boring a few enticing holes two inches in diameter, in likely sandbanks, steep road cuttings and walls, especially over water.

ROOK. *Corvus frugilegus.* Resident and generally distributed. Agricultural areas with trees for nesting.

Feeds openly on ground in small parties or flocks (a lone rook is usually a crow!). Cereals, potatoes, roots, fruit, nuts, berries, insects, worms. Will also feed on carrion (dead lambs, etc.), and kill small birds in hard weather. Comes freely to ground station for almost anything.

Nests in treetop colonies normally. Mass of sticks solidified

with earth, lined with grasses and straw. Three to five
light blue-green to green and grey-green eggs. Late March
onwards. Incubation, sixteen to eighteen days; fledging,
twenty-nine to thirty days. One brood.

Read: *The Life of the Rook*, G. K. Yeates, Allan, 1934.

JACKDAW. *Corvus monedula*. Resident and common
except in north-west Scotland. Farm and parkland, cliffs,
old buildings.

Jaunty bird, feeding in parties or flocks on animal and
vegetable matter. Will take young birds and eggs if it gets
the chance. Comes freely to bird table or ground station for
scraps, cereals, potato, fruit, berries and nuts. Fond of
macaroni-cheese.

Nests in colonies in trees, buildings, rocks or rabbit
burrows, holes, cracks or crevices; almost any hole will do
– often in bottom of rook or heron's nest. Nest of twigs,
sometimes very bulky, sometimes not. Lining of grass,
wool, hair, etc. Usually four to six eggs. Pale greenish-blue,
spotted brownish-black. Mid-April. Incubation, seventeen
to eighteen days; fledging, seventeen to eighteen days. One
brood.

Nestbox: Enclosed type, with not less than 6 in. entrance
hole, 17 in. interior depth, at least 7½ in. square floor. Or
open type as for kestrel.

Read: *King Solomon's Ring*, Konrad Lorenz, Methuen,
1952.

MAGPIE. *Pica pica*. Resident and generally distributed
in England and Wales, scarce in parts of Scotland. Farmland and open country with hedges and trees.

Frequently in pairs or small parties foraging on ground
and in hedgerows for insects, small mammals and birds.
Cereals, fruit, nuts, peas and berries. Will come nervously
to bird table or ground station for large scraps, which it
takes away. Fond of the milk bottle. Not to be welcomed
because of its predatory habits in the breeding season.

Nests in tall trees, thorny bush or neglected hedgerow.
Bulky, domed structure of sticks, with an inner lining
of earth and roots. Five to eight eggs, greenish-blue to

yellowish and greyish-green, spotted and mottled brown and ash. April onwards. Incubation, seventeen to eighteen days; fledging, about twenty-two to twenty-seven days. One brood.

JAY. *Garrulus glandarius*. Resident and generally distributed. Woodland, never far from trees.

Hops about branches and on ground. Mostly vegetable food, peas, potatoes, corn, beechmast, nuts, fruit and berries. Animal food includes eggs and small birds, mice, slugs, snails, worms and insects. Eats large numbers of acorns and, like other crows, has the habit of burying acorns and other surplus food in secret places in trees and underground. Shy bird, except in some well-timbered suburban areas where it becomes very tame and will come to the bird table or ground station for almost any food.

Nests fairly low in undergrowth or tree-fork. Sticks and twigs and a little earth, lined with roots and perhaps hair. Five or six sage-green or olive-buff eggs, mottled with darker olive spots. Early May. Incubation, sixteen to seventeen days; fledging, twenty days. One brood.

GREAT TIT. *Parus major*. Resident and generally distributed, scarcer in northern Scotland. Woodland, hedges, gardens.

Forages in trees and hedgerows for insects, spiders, worms. Fruit, peas, nuts and seeds. Does some damage to buds in spring, but it was once estimated that one pair of great tits will destroy 7,000 to 8,000 insects, mainly caterpillars, in about three weeks. Fierce bird that will attack and eat a bee. Comes freely to bird table, to hoppers and scrap baskets, where it will display its acrobatic powers as it takes coconut, peanuts, hemp and other seeds, meat, fat, suet, pudding and cheese. May help itself to cream off the top of your milk bottle if you leave it too long on the doorstep.

Nests in trees or wall holes or crevices. Also in second-hand nests, or the foundations of larger nests. If no natural sites are available it may use letter-boxes, flower-pots, beehives, and almost any kind of hole. Nest lined with a thick layer of hair or down. Five to eleven white eggs, splotched with reddish-brown. End April to June. Incubation, thirteen to fourteen days; fledging, about three weeks. One brood.

Nestbox: Enclosed type, with 1⅛ in. diameter entrance hole, interior depth at least 5 in. from hole, floor at least 4 in. square.

Read: *Birds as Individuals*, Len Howard, Collins, 1952.

BLUE TIT. *Parus caeruleus.* Resident and generally distributed except in north-west Scotland. Woodland, hedges, gardens.

Forages in trees, hedgerows and around houses. Wheat, nuts, seeds and insects. Damage to buds and ripe fruit outweighed by consumption of insects. Pugnacious, will hold insect prey with its feet and dismember with bill almost like a hawk. Confiding species that will come readily to bird feeding stations for almost anything. Milk-drinker, as great tit.

Nests as great tit. Seven to fourteen white eggs usually spotted with light chestnut. Late April /May. Incubation thirteen to fourteen days; fledging, fifteen to twenty-one days. One brood.

Nestbox: Enclosed, with 1 in. to 1⅛ in. entrance hole, interior as great tit.

Read: *Birds as Individuals*, Len Howard, Collins.

COAL TIT. *Parus ater.* Resident and generally distributed. Wooded country and gardens with a preference for conifers. Not so commonly found in orchards and hedgerows.

Forages in trees, especially conifers, for insects and spiders. On ground, for seeds and nuts. Not quite so common at bird tables as great and blue tits, but will take the same foods.

Nests in trees, walls or bank holes close to ground. Moss with thick layer of hair or down and feathers. Seven to eleven white eggs with reddish-brown spots. Late April and May. Incubation, seventeen to eighteen days; fledging, sixteen days. Usually one brood.

Nestbox: as blue tit.

CRESTED TIT. *Parus cristatus.* Resident in a few parts of north-east Scotland only. Pine woods and forests.

Forages mainly on tree trunks for insects, ripe pine cone seeds, berries. Will come to feed at tit-bell and, sometimes, at bird table.

Nests in holes or crevices in old and decayed pine stumps, also in alders and birches, and sometimes in fencing posts. Dead moss lined with hair of deer or hare, sometimes feathers or wool. Five to six white eggs splotched with chestnut-red. End April/May. Incubation, fourteen to fifteen days; fledging, seventeen to eighteen days. One brood.

Nestbox: Enclosed. $1\frac{1}{8}$ in. to $1\frac{1}{2}$ in. entrance hole. Interior depth not less than 5 in., floor not less than 4 in. square.

MARSH TIT. *Parus palustris.* Resident and widespread in most of England and Wales, but not in Scotland or Ireland. Deciduous woods, hedgerows, thickets and sometimes in gardens, but likes to be near woodland, and not, as might be imagined, marshes.

Forages over trees for insects; on ground for weed seeds, beechmast, berries and sunflower seeds. Comes to bird table and hanging devices for food as blue tit.

Nests in holes in willows, alders, etc., and sometimes in walls. Moss with lining of hair or down. Seven to eight white eggs, spotted with red-brown. End April and May. Incubation, thirteen days; fledging sixteen to seventeen days. Possibly two broods.

Nestbox: as blue tit.

WILLOW TIT. *Parus atricapillus.* Resident. Fairly frequent in parts of south-east England, scattered locally elsewhere. Marshy or damp woods, hedges and thickets.

Forages over trees and on ground for insects, spiders and berries. Will come to bird table for seeds, peanuts.

Excavates a nest chamber in soft, rotten wood – usually in birch, willow or alder. Pad of down mixed with wood-fibre, some feathers. Eight or nine white eggs usual, spotted with brown-red. Late April and May. Incubation, thirteen days; fledging, seventeen to nineteen days. Probably one brood.

Nestbox: Titbox stuffed with sawdust, or fix rotten birch /alder log to tree low down in suitable place.

LONG-TAILED TIT. *Aegithalos caudatus.* Resident and generally distributed except in very barren districts and islands. Thickets, bushy heaths, coppices and hedgerows. Also woods in winter.

Feeds in trees, rarely on ground, restlessly searching for insects and seeds. Comes infrequently to gardens and bird

tables, except in hard weather when it will come to hanging devices for suet and pudding.

Nest in bushes, furze or brambles, sometimes in trees. Large egg-shaped nest of moss woven with cobwebs and hair with a lining of many feathers. Entrance hole near top. Eight to twelve eggs, sometimes unmarked, sometimes a cap of spots or freckles, March, April. Incubation, fourteen to eighteen days; fledging, fifteen to sixteen days. Normally one brood.

NUTHATCH. *Sitta europae.* Resident and fairly common in Wales and southern England. Old trees in woods, parkland and gardens.

Dodges about on tree trunks. Wedges nuts, acorns, beechmast and seeds in crevices, and hacks them open with bill. Also takes insects. Will come freely to bird table and hanging devices for hemp, seeds, nuts, cake, fat, etc. Try jamming a brazil nut into a crevice.

Nests in tree-hole or sometimes in wall-hole. Female fills crevices and reduces entrance hole to desired size with mud.

Nest lined with flakes of bark or leaves. Six to eleven white eggs spotted with red-brown. End April to June. Incubation, fourteen to fifteen days; fledging, about twenty-four days. Usually one brood.

Nestbox: Enclosed, $1\frac{1}{8}$ in. to $1\frac{1}{2}$ in. entrance hole. Interior depth not less than 5 in., floor not less than 4 in. square.

TREE CREEPER. *Certhia familiaris.* Resident and generally distributed. Woodland, parks, gardens with large trees.

Forages unobtrusively for insects over trees. Does not come to bird table, but may indulge in crushed nuts and porridge spread in crevices of rough-barked trees, especially Wellingtonia.

Nests behind loose bark or cracks on tree trunks or behind ivy. Sometimes in wall or building crevices. Twigs, moss, grass, lined with feathers and bits of wool. Usually six white eggs with red-brown spots at big end. End April to June. Incubation, fourteen to fifteen days; fledging, fourteen to fifteen days. May be second brood.

Nestbox: May come to enclosed type, or see BTO guide, *Nestboxes*, for special designs.

WREN. *Troglodytes troglodytes.* Resident and generally distributed. Gardens, thickets, woods, rockbanks. Avoids the centres of large towns.

Lives in a world of cracks and crevices, twigs and woodpiles, hedgebottoms, and the mysterious undergrowth round fallen trees. Active and diligent hunter for insects and spiders. Will take crumbs, but is not a common bird table visitor.

Nests in hedges, holes in trees, banks or buildings. Cock bird makes several nests of moss, grass, leaves, etc., and the hen lines the final choice with feathers. Five to six eggs, white spotted with brownish-red. Incubation, fourteen to fifteen days; fledging, sixteen to seventeen days. Usually two broods.

Nestbox: May take to one of the standard enclosed types, but is much more likely to find a natural or semi-natural place such as a faggot-pile or creeper-clad wall.

Read: *The Wren*, Edward A. Armstrong, Collins, 1955.

MISTLE THRUSH (Stormcock). *Turdus viscivorus*. Resident and generally distributed, except in high mountains and treeless districts. Large gardens, orchards, woods.

Feeds mainly on ground, although it likes to sing from the highest point of a tree. Thrives on berries and fruit without conflicting with gardeners' interests. Yew and rowan especially, but also hawthorn, holly, mistletoe, juniper, rose and ivy. All wild fruits except blackberry. Will come to ground station, less freely to bird table, sultanas, currants, and bird pudding. Very partial to bird garden life without being particularly friendly to man.

Nests usually in tree fork or on bough. Grasses, moss, etc. Strengthened with earth and lined with fine grasses, the rim ornamented with lichens, bits of wool, feathers, etc. Four tawny-cream to greenish-blue eggs, splotched with brown and lilac. February to April. Incubation, thirteen to fourteen days; fledging, fourteen to sixteen days. Frequently two broods.

FIELDFARE. *Turdus pilaris*. Winter visitor, generally distributed. Open country, fields and hedges.

Flocks feed in open formation across fields, looking for slugs, spiders, insects. In hedgerows, for berries of hawthorn, holly and rowan, yew, etc. In hard weather will come to ground station or bird table for berries, fruit, seeds, pudding, etc.

Breeds in Scandinavia, Central and Eastern Europe and Siberia.

SONG THRUSH. *Turdus ericetorum*. Resident and generally distributed. Parks, woods, hedges, shrubberies and gardens, especially around human habitation.

Forages in open and in undergrowth for worms, slugs and especially snails, which it smashes on 'anvil' stones. Also insects, windfalls, berries and seeds. Will eat soft fruit, but is beneficial on the whole. Somewhat nervous visitor to ground station, not so often on bird table, fond of sultanas, also currants, cheese, fat, apples and scraps.

Nests in hedgerows, bushes, trees, among ivy, occasionally in buildings. Strongly-built of grasses, roots, etc. Stiffened with mud and with a unique lining of rotten wood or dung mixed with saliva and moulded into shape by the hen's breast. Four to five eggs, blue with greenish tinge, spotted black or red-brown. March to August. Incubation, thirteen to fourteen days; fledging, thirteen to fourteen days. Two or three broods.

REDWING. *Turdus musicus.* Winter visitor, generally distributed. Open country and open woods.

Feeds in loose flocks in field or woods. Worms, slugs, snails, insects. Hawthorn, holly, rowan, yew berries. In hard weather will come to ground station or bird table for berries, seeds, scraps, fruit, etc.

Breeds in Scandinavia, Eastern Europe and Siberia.

BLACKBIRD. *Turdus merula.* Resident and generally distributed. Woods, hedges, gardens, shrubberies.

Feeds in open and in undergrowth, but never far from cover. Makes surprising amount of noise as it searches among dead leaves. Insects, worms (which it often steals from a song-thrush), fruit, berries and seeds. Will come freely to ground station and to bird table, for sultanas especially, cheese, fat, apples, cake, 'Rice Krispies', berries, seeds.

Nests in hedges, bushes, evergreens and ivy, sometimes in outhouses. Nest like song-thrush, but the mud cup is lined with grasses. Four to five eggs, bluish-green freckled with red-brown. February (or even earlier) to July. Incubation, thirteen to fourteen days; fledging, thirteen to fourteen days. Two or three broods.

Nestbox: Tray or open-fronted type, with a floor area 12 in. square.

Read: *A Study of Blackbirds*, D. W. Snow, Allen and Unwin, 1958.

REDSTART. *Phoenicurus phoenicurus.* Summer resident, widely distributed but local. Woodlands, parks, bushy commons with old trees, ruins, orchards, well-timbered gardens.

Restless bird, flitting amongst branches or hawking for insects. Might come to bird table for berries, fruit and mincemeat.

Hole-nester, tree or stump, buildings, walls, outhouses, rocks, quarries. Nest made of grasses, strips of bark, mosses, roots, and lined with hair and feathers. About six pale blue eggs. May onwards. Incubation, fourteen days; fledging, fourteen days. Frequently two broods.

Nestbox: Enclosed. Entrance hole $1\frac{1}{8}$ in. to 2 in. diameter, inside depth not less than 5 in. from hole, floor not less than 4 in. square.

Read: *The Redstart*, John Buxton, Collins, 1950.

BLACK REDSTART. *Phoenicurus ochruros.* Passage-migrant and winter visitor, some staying to breed in southern England. Cliffs, large old buildings, rocky and 'waste' ground such as building-sites, dumps or ruins.

Restless bird, in trees, over buildings, and on ground. Hawks for insects. Also takes berries. Although it lives amongst us, it is independent of our food, yet surely it might come to a feeding station for minced meat or berries, especially in hard weather.

Nests in crevices and holes of rocks or buildings, or on rafters, under eaves in outbuildings. Loosely-made of grass, moss, fibre, etc., lined with hair and feathers. Four to six white eggs. Early April onward. Incubation, twelve to thirteen days; fledging, sixteen to eighteen days. Two broods.

ROBIN. *Erithacus rubecula.* Resident and generally distributed, except in extreme north of Scotland. Gardens, hedgerows, woods with undergrowth.

Feeds freely in open and in undergrowth. Insects, spiders, worms, weed seeds, fruit, berries. Has a flattering relationship with man and will follow the digging spade hopefully. Enthusiastic bird-tabler, very fond of mealworms, will also take seeds, nuts, oats, pudding, etc. Fond of butter and margarine, and is alleged to be able to tell the difference! Unsociable bird, it will endure the close company of its relations at the bird table only in hungry times.

Nests in gardens and hedgerows in bankside hollows, tree holes, walls, amongst creeper, on shelves in out-buildings, often at foot of bush or grassy tuft. Foundation of dead leaves and moss, neatly lined with hair and perhaps a feather or two. Five or six eggs usually. White with sandy or reddish freckles. Late March onward. Incubation, thirteen to fourteen days; fledging, twelve to fourteen days. Two broods.

Nestbox: Old tin or kettle. Ledge or tray, open-fronted box. Interior floor at least 4 in. square.

Read: *The Life of the Robin*, David Lack, Witherby, 1965.

BLACKCAP. *Sylvia atricapilla.* Summer resident, frequently winters, local but fairly distributed, except in remote north and west. Open woodland, thickly bushy places, gardens with trees.

Active bird, searching in cover for insects, fruit and berries. Not often on ground. Will come to bird table for a wide range of food, including rolled oats, berries, crumbs and scraps.

Nests in bushes (especially snowberry), hedgerows, evergreens. Stems, roots and grasses, lined with finer grass and hair. Five eggs, light buff or stone ground, blotched brown and ashy. Mid-May onward. Incubation, ten to eleven days; fledging, ten to thirteen days. Often two broods.

GOLDCREST. *Regulus regulus.* Resident and generally distributed except in remote north-west. Woods, coniferous gardens, hedgerows.

Active and tame bird, which flits from twig to twig searching for spiders and insects. Will come to bird table and to hanging fat.

Nests in thick foliage of conifer. Ball of moss lined with feathers; held together by spiders' webs and suspended from branch. Seven to ten white/ochreous eggs, spotted brown. End April to early June. Incubation, about sixteen days; fledging, about eighteen to twenty days. Two broods.

SPOTTED FLYCATCHER. *Muscicapa striata*. Summer resident, generally distributed. Gardens, parks, woodland edges.

Sits on an exposed perch, flits out frequently to hawk after flying insects.

Nests against wall or on small ledge supported by creeper or fruit tree, etc. Moss and grass, lined with wool, hair and feathers. Four to five greenish grey eggs with brown spots. Mid-May to June. Incubation, twelve to thirteen days; fledging, twelve to thirteen days. One brood.

Nestbox: Ledge or open-fronted box with a 3 in. square floor.

PIED FLYCATCHER. *Muscicapa hypoleuca*. Summer resident locally in parts of Great Britain. Woods, parks, gardens, usually near water.

Catches insects in flight by hawking, but also takes them from trees and on the ground. Worms and berries occasionally.

Nests in holes of trees, walls. Bark, leaves, grasses with a lining of fibres and grass. Four to seven pale blue eggs. Mid-May. Incubation, twelve to thirteen days; fledging, thirteen days. One brood.

Nestbox: Enclosed. Entrance hole $1\frac{1}{8}$ in. to $1\frac{1}{2}$ in. diameter, interior depth not less than 5 in., floor not less than 4 in. square.

DUNNOCK (Hedge Sparrow). *Prunella modularis*. Resident and generally distributed. Gardens, shrubberies, hedgerows.

Forages unobtrusively on ground among dead leaves, hedgerow bottoms, etc. Weed seeds in winter, insects in summer. Will come freely to ground station, less readily to bird table for crumbs of cornflakes, cake, biscuit, seeds. Unlike most other birds will eat lentils.

Nests in hedges and evergreens, faggot heaps. Twigs, moss, leaves, etc., lined with moss, hair and feathers. Four to five deep blue eggs. April onward. Incubation, twelve days; fledging, twelve days. Two broods. Often serves as host to cuckoo.

ROCK PIPIT. *Anthus spinoletta*. Resident and generally distributed. Rocky shores in summer; marshes, waterways, estuaries and coasts in winter.

Forages near water for insects, animals and vegetable matter. Will come freely to a ground feeding station near the shore for crumbs, scraps, cheese.

Nests in hole or cliff-crevice close to the shore. Stems and grasses, lined with grass and hair. Four to five greyish-white eggs spotted olive-brown and ashy-grey. Late April to June. Incubation, about fourteen days; fledging, sixteen days. Two broods.

PIED WAGTAIL. *Motacilla alba*. Resident and generally distributed. Gardens, farms, buildings and cultivated country.

Lively bird—feeds over ground, but often flutters up to take an insect. Mainly insects, fond of shallow pool edges. Will come freely to ground feeding station, scavenging crumbs and scraps where other birds have left unconsidered trifles.

Nests in holes and on ledges of walls, outhouses, creeper, banks and cliffs. Leaves, twigs, stems lined with hair, wool and feathers. Five or six eggs, greyish or bluish-white, spotted grey-brown and grey. Late April to June. Incubation, thirteen to fourteen days; fledging, fourteen to fifteen days. Two broods. Often host to cuckoo.

Nestbox: Ledge or open-fronted box, with a floor area of not less than 4 in. square. Fix it in a stone wall: or make a cavity behind a loose stone which can be used as an inspection door.

STARLING. *Sturnus vulgaris*. Resident and generally distributed. Found almost anywhere, having successfully adapted itself to man's ways.

Active bird, foraging on ground and in trees and hawking for insects. Animal and vegetable foods of almost any kind. Enthusiastic bird table and ground station visitor.

Sometimes defeated by hanging devices. Very fond of fresh
creamy milk and leg-of-lamb bones, particularly marrow,
but will eat anything available.

Nests, often in colonies, in tree or building holes. Untidy
structure of straw and grasses lined with feathers. Five to
seven pale blue eggs. End March onwards. Incubation,
twelve to thirteen days; fledging, twenty to twenty-two
days. One brood usually.

Nestbox: Enclosed. Entrance hole 2 in. diameter, inside
depth 12 in., floor area 9 in. by 9 in. Starlings will sometimes take over an *old* titbox, when the wood has softened
enough to enable them to hack away at the hole and enlarge
it.

HAWFINCH. *Coccothraustes coccothraustes.* Resident, generally distributed, but not much in evidence; local in Great
Britain, but very rare in Ireland. Woodland, parks, orchards
and wooded gardens.

Feeds in trees, taking kernels and seeds. Fond of green
peas. Will come shyly to bird table for fruit, seeds and nuts.
Highly-developed bill muscles enable it to crack cherry and
plum stones, etc., to extract the kernel.

Nests on fruit tree branches or in bushes and other trees.
Foundation of twigs supports shallow cup of lichens, moss,
grass lined thinly with roots and hair. Four to six eggs,
ground colour light bluish or greyish-green spotted and
streaked blackish-brown. Late April onwards. Incubation,
nine-and-a-half days; fledging, ten to eleven days. Occasionally two broods.

Read: *The Hawfinch*, Guy Mountfort, Collins, 1957.

GREENFINCH. *Chloris chloris.* Resident and common.
Gardens, shrubberies, farmland.

Feeds sociably on ground and in trees. Seeds of all kinds,
berries, fruit tree buds, occasionally beetles, ants, aphids.
Comes to bird table and seed hoppers for all seeds, peanut
and sunflower especially. Will even eat buckwheat. Berries
of yew, ivy, hawthorn, elder, etc.

Nests in hedgerows and evergreen bushes and trees. Moss
interwoven with twigs and lined with roots and hair,

sometimes feathers. Four to six eggs, ground colour dirty white to pale greenish-blue, variably spotted red-brown. Late April/May onwards. Incubation, thirteen to fourteen days; fledging, thirteen to sixteen days. Two broods.

GOLDFINCH. *Carduelis carduelis*. Resident and generally distributed. Gardens, orchards and cultivated land.

Small flocks flitter around plant seed-heads, not so much on the ground. Seeds, especially thistle, teazle and other weeds. Also insects. Will come occasionally to the bird table for small seeds of grains and grasses. Crack some hemp for them, as their beaks are not as strong as those of other finches.

Nests especially in fruit trees and chestnuts. Also in hedges and thick berberis. Elegant nest of roots, grass, moss and lichens, lined with vegetable down and wool, placed far out at the end of the branch. Five to six bluish-white eggs, spotted and streaked red-brown. Early May onwards. Incubation, twelve to thirteen days; fledging, thirteen to fourteen days. Two broods.

BULLFINCH. *Pyrrhula pyrrhula*. Resident and generally distributed. Shrubberies, copses, gardens, orchards, hedge-rows.

In autumn and early winter eats mainly weed seeds, some berries; in a hard winter, if its natural food, ashmast, is short it will ravage fruit tree buds. Remedy is to spread 'Transweb' (Transatlantic Plastics Ltd, Ventnor, I.o.W.) among branches of smaller trees and shrubs. Unsightly but effective. Not keen on bird tables, may occasionally come for seeds and berries.

Nests in hedges, evergreen bushes, creeper, brambles. Foundation of twig and moss, cup lined with interlacing roots and hair. Four to five green-blue eggs with few purple-brown spots and streaks. Late April onwards. Incubation, twelve to fourteen days; fledging, twelve to seventeen days. At least two broods.

CROSSBILL. *Loxia curvirostra*. Late summer visitor. Varying numbers. Every few years invades and over-winters in great numbers, many individuals remaining to breed. Coniferous woods, gardens and parks.

Clambers about branches parrot-fashion in parties, wrenching off pine and larch cones. Holds cone in foot while it splits the scales and extracts the seed with its tongue. Apart from cone seeds, will eat thistle seeds, berries and insects. Very tame, it will visit bird table for seeds, especially sunflower. Very fond of water and bathing.

Nests on pine branches. Foundation of twigs, cups of moss, grass and wool lined with grass, fur, hair, feathers. Four greenish-white eggs with few spots /streaks of purple-red. January to July. Incubation, twelve to thirteen days; fledging, more than twenty-four days.

CHAFFINCH. *Fringilla coelebs*. Resident and widely distributed. Gardens, hedgerows, woods, commons, farmland.

Forages on ground and in trees. Insects, spiders, fruit, fruit buds. Tame and enthu-siastic bird-tabler, taking seeds of all kinds, bird pudding, scraps and berries.

Nests in hedgerows, orchards, gardens, not choosy. Beautiful structure of moss with interwoven grass and roots, decorated with lichens held together by spiders' webs. Lined with hair and feathers. Four to five greenish-blue to brownish-stone eggs, spotted / streaked purplish-brown. Mid-April to June. Incubation, eleven to thirteen days; fledging, thirteen to fourteen days.

YELLOWHAMMER (Yellow Bunting). *Emberiza citri-nella*. Resident and generally distributed. Farmland with hedgerows or bushy cover, bushy commons and heaths. Very common along roadsides.

Feeds mainly on ground, hopping and pecking for corn, weed seeds, wild fruits (including blackberries, which most birds don't like), leaves, grasses. Insects, spiders, worms, etc. Will come to garden seed-hopper once it has discovered it, but not really a garden bird.

Great spotted wood-
pecker feeding from the
hand

In very dry spring
weather pour some
water into a convenient
dust bowl so that the
house martins can col-
lect mud for their nests
▼

Juvenile robins, not long out of the nest. Don't 'rescue' them, they are not lost!

Try jamming a brazil nut into an old tree stump or crevice for a nuthatch

Great tit feeding from the hand

An artificial robin's nest like this should be placed about five feet off the ground, shaded from direct sun, and with a hole to drain any rainwater

In hard weather birds fluff out their feathers and trap a warm layer of air against their bodies. This robin appears well-fed and fat, though in fact it is probably badly in need of food and water

The first myrtle warbler to be spotted in Great Britain revealed itself by coming to this bird table in the winter of 1954/55. An American bird, it crossed the Atlantic after being blown off course by strong winds

Nests in bottom of hedgerow or bush. Straw, grass, stalks, moss-lined with hair and grass. Three to four eggs, whitish to purplish to brownish-red with dark brown hairlines and spots. Late April to August or later. Incubation, twelve to fourteen days; fledging, twelve to thirteen days. Two or three broods.

HOUSE SPARROW. *Passer domesticus.* Resident and widely distributed. Cultivated land and vicinity of human habitation.

Operates in non-territorial 'gangs', cleaning up wherever there are easy pickings on farms, hedgerows, parks, gardens, docks, railways, and 'waste' land of all kinds. Corn, seeds, insects. Tough customer at the bird table, eating almost anything, especially cereal-based foods. Wastes a great deal. Much too successful; where there are too many sparrows other birds tend to get crowded out.

Nests in holes or niches around occupied houses; eaves, drainpiping, creeper, also in hedges and trees, house-martins' nests, or in the foundations of rooks' nests. Untidy structure of straw and grasses lined with feathers and odd-ments. In cramped locations may consist of lining only. Three to five greyish-white eggs, finely spotted grey and brown. May to August. Incubation, twelve to fourteen days; fledging, fifteen days. Two to three broods.

Nestbox: Enclosed. Entrance hole $1\frac{1}{4}$ in. diameter, inside depth not less than 5 in., floor 6 in. square. May easily become a pest, denying nestboxes to more welcome birds. Drastic solution is to destroy nests as soon as they are built.

Read: *The House Sparrow*, J. D. Summers-Smith, Collins, 1963.

TREE SPARROW. *Passer montanus.* Resident and widely-distributed in England and Wales, eastern side of Scotland and a few parts of Ireland. 'Country cousin' of house sparrows, frequenting same habitat but with less attachment to habitations.

Feeds on weed seeds, corn, insects, spiders. Will visit bird table for seeds and scraps but is a shy bird compared with the house sparrow.

T—D

Nests in holes of trees, banks, haystacks and thatch, buildings, and in foundations of disused rook or magpie nests. Untidy structure similar to house sparrow. Four to six eggs, smaller, browner, darker, than house sparrow. Late April to August. Incubation, twelve to fourteen days; fledging, twelve to fourteen days. Two broods usually.

Nestbox: Enclosed, entrance hole $1\frac{1}{8}$ in. diameter, inside depth not less than 6 in., floor not less than 4 in. square.

Appendices

A *Recipes*

I. BASIC PUD

Take seeds, peanuts, cheese, oatmeal, dry cake, and scraps. Put them in a container, pour hot fat over the mixture until it is covered, and leave to set. Turn out on to a table, unless you have prepared it in a tit-bell or coconut holder. Rough quantities: One pound of mixture to half a pound of melted fat.

2. BIRD CAKE

2 lb. self-raising flour (Allinsons); ½ lb. margarine; and a little sugar. Mix with water and bake like large rock bun.

3. ANTI-SPARROW PUDDING

Boil together for five minutes one cup of sugar and one cup of water. Mix with one cup of melted fat (suet, bacon, or ordinary shortening), and leave to cool.

Mix with breadcrumbs, flour, bird seed, a little boiled rice and scraps, until the mixture is very stiff. Then pack in any kind of tin can or glass jar. Lay the can on its side in a tree, on the window-sill, or in any place where birds can perch and pick out the food. The can must be placed securely, so that the birds cannot dislodge it nor rain get inside. May not fool sparrows for long, though.

4. MEALWORM CULTURE

Prepare a large circular biscuit tin as follows: punch small holes in the lid for ventilation, place a layer of old hessian sacking in the bottom, and sprinkle fairly thickly with bran. Put in a slice or two of bread and raw potato, followed by another two layers of sacking/bran/bread/potato, like a three-decker sandwich. You can put a raw cabbage leaf on top, if you like. Keep the tin at room temperature, not in hot sun.

Now introduce two or three hundred mealworms (buy them from a pet-shop) into the prepared tin. After a few weeks the mealworms will turn into creamy pupae, then into little black beetles. The beetles will lay eggs which hatch into mealworms, and so on. Crop as necessary. Replace bread, potato and cabbage as necessary. If you want to start new colonies, prepare another tin and transfer some bits of dry bread (these will carry beetle eggs) from the flourishing colony. If you can't face this performance, buy your mealworms from the professionals, consoling yourself with the thought that successful mealworm breeding is even more difficult than it sounds.

SUPPLIERS OF BIRD FOOD

E. W. Coombs Ltd, Cross Street Works, Chatham, Kent. Sluis Universal Bird Food; mealworms; seed mixture.

Greenrigg Works, 30 Penrith Road, Hainault, Ilford, Essex. Peanuts; birdseed; sunflower seeds; mealworms.

John E. Haith Ltd, Park Street, Cleethorpes, Lincolnshire. Haith's Wild Bird Food; tit food (in bulk); peanut kernels and shells; sunflower seeds (mixed).

Eric Wood, Ombersley, Droitwich, Worcestershire. Seed mixture; sunflower seed; peanut kernels; food blocks.

Wholefood Ltd, 112 Baker Street, London, W.1. Wheat, rye, oats, barley, rice, buckwheat and millet, whole grain grown organically without the use of chemical pesticides.

SUPPLIERS OF POND PLANTS, etc.

Queensborough Fisheries, 111 Goldhawk Road, Shepherds Bush, London, W.12. Send for list.

B *Suppliers of bird furniture, etc.*

Royal Society for the Protection of Birds, *The Lodge, Sandy, Bedfordshire*. Free catalogue on application. THE RSPB BIRD TABLE, 18 in. by 12 in., illustrated right, is

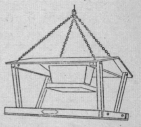

well-proportioned and well-finished. It can be hung from the branch of a tree or fitted to the top of a post, as every table comes complete with chains *and* post adaptor. The roof over-laps the table slightly and ensures that food is kept dry in most conditions, although strong winds and driving rain inevitably play havoc. But this is probably the best buy in bird-tables. The roof is fitted with rails to take a food hopper, which slides into place well sheltered. Hoppers can be very tiresome gadgets, as they are so susceptible to wind and to rain-jamming, but again this one is the most efficient I have found. Bird table 41s 6d, hopper 10s 6d, post paid.

THE NESTBOX, illustrated left, is strongly made. The top section

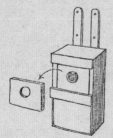

can be easily removed either for cleaning purposes or to provide the open design suit-able for robins, pied wagtails and spotted fly-catchers. The hole is drilled $1\frac{1}{8}$ in. dia-meter and is suitable for tits, tree sparrows and nuthatches. An aluminium hole-patch is available as a deterrent to woodpeckers and squirrels which might want to enlarge the holes. (Tits often peck at the holes of their nestboxes. This is perfectly normal be-haviour and is *not* because the hole is too small.) Nestbox 15s 6d, hole-patch 2s 6d, post paid.

THE FOOD BASKET, illustrated right, is suitable for dispensing nearly a pound of shelled peanuts or kitchen scraps. It has a wire lid and is free of sharp wire-ends. 7s 6d post paid.

WARNING. Avoid any peanut feeder which involves a flexible coiled spring system. These are highly dangerous, since a bird may get its feet jammed when another flies away from the feeder causing the spring to contract.

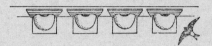

Clent House Gardens, *Clent, Worcestershire.*
ARTIFICIAL HOUSE MARTIN NESTS, illustrated above, act as a magnet to this species and encourage the establishment of a colony. The nests are fixed under the eaves of house or barn. Sometimes house sparrows may worm their way in by enlarging the holes but Clent House supply a leaflet with instructions for a simple anti-sparrow method. Incidentally this method, involving a screen of 12 in. weighted cords, 2½ in. apart, and hung 6 in. away from the entrance hole, can be used to protect natural house martin nests as well. 12s 6d post paid.

LOGNEST, illustrated right, is of silver birch, making a solid waterproof and natural nestsite for tits. 11s post paid. This firm also supply other excellent nestboxes and a 12 in. by 8 in. bird tray, price 25s, for which a wall bracket is available free on request.

Eric Wood, *Ombersley, Droitwich, Worcestershire.* This firm supplies a useful free catalogue on application. Their nestboxes cost around 15s, are available in mahogany at extra cost, and are reduced in price if you buy four or more. Bird tables of various sizes and specifications are available from 15s to 90s.

Greenrigg Works, *30 Penrith Road, Hainault, Ilford, Essex.* Catalogue 7d.

GRILLE PEANUT FEEDER, illustrated left, is a strongly-made device which holds a lot of peanuts and gives them excellent protection from rain. 18s 9d post paid. See also the smaller wire cage peanut feeder which can be attached to a window pane by means of a suction disc. 6s 9d post paid.

SPARROW-PROOF PEANUT FEEDER, illustrated page 103 left, 19s 9d p.p. TITBELL, illustrated

below centre, for feeding fat and scraps to tits and nuthatches.
12s 3d p.p. Gravity-flow WATER FEEDER BASE, for use with 1 lb. jam
jar, illustrated right. 3s 9d post paid. This firm also supplies a
varied selection of bird tables, nestboxes and gadgets of all sorts.

C *Birds which visit feeding stations*

Mallard
Canada Goose
Mute Swan
Pheasant
Moorhen
Turnstone
Herring Gull
Black-headed Gull
Wood Pigeon
Collared Dove
(Feral Pigeon)
Kingfisher
Green Woodpecker
Great Spotted Woodpecker
Lesser Spotted Woodpecker
Rook
Jackdaw
Magpie
Jay
Great Tit
Blue Tit
Coal Tit
Marsh Tit
Willow Tit
Long-tailed Tit

Nuthatch
Tree Creeper
Wren
Mistle Thrush
Fieldfare
Song Thrush
Redwing
Blackbird
Robin
Blackcap
Goldcrest
Dunnock
Rock Pipit
Pied Wagtail
Starling
Hawfinch
Greenfinch
Goldfinch
Siskin
Bullfinch
Crossbill
Chaffinch
Yellowhammer
House Sparrow
Tree Sparrow

D *Birds which use nestboxes*

Regularly
Stock Dove
Tawny Owl
Swift
Great Spotted Woodpecker
Wryneck
Jackdaw
Great Tit
Blue Tit
Coal Tit
Marsh Tit
Nuthatch
Redstart
Robin
Spotted Flycatcher
Pied Flycatcher
Starling
House Sparrow
Tree Sparrow

Occasionally
Barn Owl
Little Owl
Green Woodpecker
Swallow
House Martin
Sand Martin
Willow Tit
Tree Creeper
Wren
Blackbird
Pied Wagtail

The British Trust for Ornithology runs a Nest Record Scheme, in which the object is to collect information about the breeding behaviour of British birds. If you feel you could collect simple, but precise, information about the birds which nest in your garden, and not necessarily in nestboxes, write to the BTO, Beech Grove, Tring, Herts, for information.

E *Life-spans of wild birds*

The following figures show the *maximum recorded* life-span for an individual of each species (to the nearest year); the *average* life expectancy for wild birds is, of course, very short indeed. These are records of the exceptional individual which has managed to survive against all the odds. The figures are available as a result of the international bird-ringing schemes which have been in operation for many years now with the object of learning more about bird numbers and migrations.

If you come across a bird with a ring on its leg, send full details (ring number, date, place, species of bird, whether the bird is freshly dead or not, or if it was alive and subsequently released, and any other relevant information) to the British Trust for Ornithology, Beech Grove, Tring, Hertfordshire. In due course you will be told the place and date of its original ringing.

NOTE: The bracketed figures are certainly unrealistic. The species involved have not been ringed in large numbers and the recovery results have yet to reveal a long-lived individual.

Blackbird	10	Hoopoe	(2)
Blackcap	5	Jackdaw	14
Bullfinch	8	Jay	18
Chaffinch	10	Kestrel	16
Creeper, Tree	7	Kingfisher	4
Crossbill	(2)	Magpie	15
Dove, Collared	(3)	Mallard	20
„ Rock	6	Martin, House	6
„ Stock	8	„ Sand	7
Dunnock	8	Moorhen	11
Fieldfare	5	Nuthatch	9
Flycatcher, Pied	9	Owl, Barn	15
„ Spotted	8	„ Little	16
Goldcrest	3	„ Tawny	17
Goldfinch	8	Pheasant	9
Goose, Canada	11	Pigeon, Wood	14
Greenfinch	10	Pipit, Rock	9
Gull, Black-headed	30	Redstart	7
„ Herring	32	Redstart, Black	(2)
Hawfinch	(2)	Redwing	19

Robin	11	Tit, Great	10
Rook	20	,, Long-tailed	4
Starling	20	,, Marsh	10
Sparrow, House	11	,, Willow	8
,, Tree	10	Turnstone	20
Swallow	16	Wagtail, Grey	(3)
Swan, Mute	19	,, Pied	6
Swift	21	Woodpecker,	
Thrush, Mistle	10	Great Spotted	9
,, Song	14	,, Green	5
Tit, Blue	10	,, Lesser Spotted	?
,, Coal	5	Wren	5
,, Crested	5	Wryneck	4
		Yellowhammer	7

F *Treatment of casualties*

1. *Orphaned or exhausted birds.* First of all, be sure the bird is really in need of help. Youngsters of some species leave the nest before they are really able to fly and hang around in hedge bottoms and in odd corners waiting to be fed. This is perfectly normal and you should leave the birds to get on with the job. Every year, hundreds of unfortunate baby blackbirds and tawny owls get 'rescued' before they are lost.

If you know definitely that the bird is not being fed, then you may decide to act as foster-parent. This can be a long and tedious job, especially in the case of a very young bird. Be very sure that you are prepared to devote a great deal of time and patience to the job before you begin. If you're not absolutely certain you can see it through then the humane action is to kill the bird. Don't condemn it to a few days or weeks of misery before it dies. As well as time and patience you will need a suitable place to keep the patient. Keep it in a warm and draught-free place. Feed with a mixture of swatted-fly, small smooth green caterpillars (not hairy ones) and finely-minced raw meat from the end of a matchstick. (Birds of prey must also have roughage, dead mice for instance.) Handle the bird very gently. Do not feed live food – always kill insects before offering them. Feed once every hour and make sure the crop is full (you can see the food stockpile and swell at the base of the throat).

It is difficult to overfeed a young bird, and it will tell you in no uncertain fashion when it is hungry. It needs no water. Do not 'pet' it, warmth and a cosy 'nest' will substitute for its mother. Keep its nest clean and dispose of its droppings promptly. As it gets older, encourage it to fly to you for food. Then take it into the garden and help it to fend for itself by planting caterpillars, etc., and 'discovering' them with it. The bird should be independent of you within a month.

An adult bird is certainly in need of help *if you can pick it up*. An exhausted or starved adult should be put in a box with a carpet of newspaper and a perch-stick low down across the floor. Give it a shallow bowl of water and a shallow bowl of food. Budgerigar mixture for seed-eaters; live insects, chopped worms, caterpillars, supplemented with packet 'insectivorous' food from a pet-shop for insect-eaters. (Soaked bread may be used for a first emergency feed, but *no* alcohol.) Leave it undisturbed in the warm (up to 70°F). Put a light on for a few hours; this will stimulate it to feed.

If the bird is still alive next day you can either let it go or continue treatment, depending on how lively it is.

2. *Injured birds.* These should be taken to the nearest vet., RSPCA or PDSA establishment. Only if you are prevented by some powerful reason from taking this course should you attempt to treat the bird yourself.

Read: *Bird Doctor*, by Katharine Tottenham, published by Nelson; and *Treatment of Sick and Wounded Birds*, by F. B. Lake, published by the British Trust for Ornithology, Beech Grove, Tring, Hertfordshire, price 8d.

G *Organizations concerned with bird life*

The Royal Society for the Protection of Birds, The Lodge, Sandy, Bedfordshire.

Illustrated journal *Birds*, free to members. Manages a network of bird reserves, organizes many exhibitions and meetings, is much concerned with conservation and with the enforcement of the Protection of Birds Act. All bird-watchers should support this society. (Send for brochure.) Junior section: *The Young Ornithologists' Club*, for boys and girls up to the age of eighteen. Organizes bird courses at hostels and observatories. Issues quarterly magazine *Bird Life* with competitions and instructive articles.

The British Trust for Ornithology, Beech Grove, Tring, Hertfordshire.

Minimum membership age, fifteen years. Members may take part in organized field studies, ringing and census work. Issues quarterly journal, *Bird Study*, six-weekly *BTO News*, invaluable field guides and other publications. Works closely with RSPB collecting evidence of harmful effects of toxic chemicals. Lending library. All serious bird-watchers should join. (Send for brochure.)

The British Ornithologists' Union, c/o The Bird Room, British Museum (Natural History), Cromwell Road, London, S.W.7.

Senior bird society in Great Britain; its main object is the advancement of ornithological science on a world scale. Quarterly journal, *The Ibis*.

The Wildfowl Trust, Slimbridge, Gloucestershire.

Illustrated annual report and periodical bulletins; maintains unique collection of swans, ducks and geese from all parts of the world.

The International Council for Bird Preservation (British Section), British Museum (Natural History), Cromwell Road, London, S.W.7.

Issues annual report, co-ordinates and promotes international bird conservation.

The Henry Doubleday Research Association, 20 Convent Lane, Bocking, Braintree, Essex.

Issues newsletters and occasional publications of vital interest to the bird gardener. Initiates research into organic farming and gardening methods; pest control without poisons.

OTHER IMPORTANT SOCIETIES CONCERNED WITH ALL
ASPECTS OF NATURAL HISTORY

International Union for Conservation of Nature and Natural Resources,
1110 Morges, Switzerland.

The Fauna Preservation Society, c/o The Zoological Society of
London, Regent's Park, London, N.W.1.

The Council for Nature, 41 Queen's Gate, Knightsbridge, London,
S.W.7.

Intelligence Unit provides important source for information.

The Society for the Promotion of Nature Reserves, c/o British Museum
(Natural History), Cromwell Road, London, S.W.7.

'Umbrella' organization co-ordinating the work of the County
Trusts for Nature Conservation.

PERIODICAL

British Birds, published monthly by H. F. and G. Witherby,
Ltd, 61/62 Watling Street, London, E.C.4. A bird-watchers'
journal; not too scientific, not too 'pop'; includes monthly report
on migrants and rarities.

H *Birds and the law*

With certain exceptions, all wild birds, their nests and eggs, are protected by law. Under certain provisions of the Protection of Birds Act, 1954, persons guilty of an offence under the Act may be liable to a fine of up to £25 and/or one month's imprisonment in respect of each offence.

Although the present Act, in repealing fifteen previous ones, represents a considerable simplification of the situation that existed before 1954, it is still by no means easy for a layman to understand. The Royal Society for the Protection of Birds has published a free leaflet which explains the Act in plain language. If you believe the law to have been broken, make detailed notes of the occurrence and contact the nearest inspector of the RSPCA or, in Scotland, Animal Welfare Society.

Read: *The Protection of Birds Act* (9d); *Statutory Instruments* (2d each), HMSO, Kingsway, London, W.C.2.

Wild Birds and the Law (simplified unofficial version of the Act). RSPB, The Lodge, Sandy, Bedfordshire. Free leaflet.

I *Birdsong recordings*

To the best of my knowledge, no one has yet published a gramophone record devoted to the songs of grateful bird-table customers. The following is a short list of useful and reasonably relevant discs.

The Country Sings: 7 inch, 45 rpm. Lawrence C. Shove, Copplestone, Dunsford, Exeter, Devon. (Send 13s.)

Mistle thrush, song thrush, rook, blackbird, great tit, wren, nuthatch, buzzard, great spotted woodpecker, green woodpecker, chiffchaff, willow warbler, tree pipit, garden warbler, blackcap, nightingale.

British Garden Birds: two 7 inch, 33⅓ rpm records included with a short book by Peter Conder, illustrated by H. J. Slijper. Recordings by A. G. Field. Published by Record Books and obtainable from the RSPB, Sandy, Beds. (26s 6d, post free.)

Typical song and calls of twenty-five garden birds, with accompanying text description of the habits of each species.

Listen ... the birds: nine 7 inch, 33⅓ rpm records (12s each, post free). RSPB, Sandy, Beds.

Witherby's Sound Guide to British Birds, H. F. and G. Witherby Ltd, 61/62 Watling Street, London, E.C.4. A guide to 115 species on the British List.

Bibliography

ATKINSON-WILLES, G. L. (1963). *Wildfowl in Great Britain;* Her Majesty's Stationery Office.

BANNERMAN, D. A. (1953–1963). *The Birds of the British Isles;* Oliver & Boyd Ltd.

BATTEN, H. M. (1933). *How to Feed and Attract the Wild Birds;* The Moray Press.

BLOTZHEIM, U. G. von (1965). Longevity Records of Swiss Birds, *The Ring*, *42*: 104–6.

BOSWALL, J. H. R. (1964). A discography of Palearctic bird sound recordings; Witherby.

CAMPBELL, B. (1952). *Bird-Watching for Beginners;* Penguin Books.

— (1953). *Finding Nests;* Collins.

CLEGG, J. (1965). *The Observers' Book of Pond Life;* Warne.

COHEN, E. (1963). *Nestboxes;* BTO, Tring, Herts.

DRABBLE, P. (1964). *The Penguin Book of Pets;* Penguin Books.

FISHER, J. (1940). *Watching Birds;* Penguin Books.

FISHER, J. and LOCKLEY, R. M. (1954). *Seabirds;* Collins.

FISHER, J. and PETERSON, R. T. (1964). *The World of Birds;* Macdonald.

FITTER, R. S. R. (1959). *The Pocket Guide to Nests and Eggs;* Collins.

FLOWER, S. S. (1938). Further Notes on the Duration of Life in Animals, IV. Birds. *Proc. Zool. Soc. Lond. 108 (Ser. A)* 195–235.

FULLER-MAITLAND, E. (1927). *Small Bird Sanctuaries;* RSPB.

HARTLEY, P. H. T. (1957). *The Bird Garden;* RSPB.

HIESEMANN, M. (English edn. 1908). *How to Attract and Protect Wild Birds;* Witherby.

HILLS, L. D. (1964). *Pest Control Without Poisons;* Henry Doubleday Research Assoc.

— (1965). *Hedgehogs and the Gardener;* HDRA.

HOLLOM, P. A. D. (rev. edn. 1955). *The Popular Handbook of British Birds;* Witherby.

HOWARD, L. (1952). *Birds as Individuals;* Collins.

KINNE, R. (1962). *The Complete Book of Nature Photography;* New York.

KNIGHT, M. (1954). *Bird Gardening;* Routledge & Kegan Paul.

MASSINGHAM, H. J. (1924). *Sanctuaries for Birds;* Bell.

MORETON, B. E. (1958). Beneficial Insects. *Min. of Ag. Bull. 20* H.M. Stationery Office.

Nicholson, E. M. (1951). *Birds and Men;* Collins.

Peterson, R. T., Mountfort, G. and Hollom, P. A. D. (rev. edn. 1966). *A Field Guide to the Birds of Britain and Europe;* Collins.

Rudd, R. L. (1965). *Pesticides and the Living Landscape;* Univ. of Wisconsin Press.

Rydzewski, W. (1962). Longevity of ringed birds; *The Ring, 33;* 147–52.

Smith, M. (1951). *British Amphibians and Reptiles;* Collins.

Southern, H. N. (ed.) (1964). *The Handbook of British Mammals;* Blackwell.

Thomson, A. L. (ed.) (1964). *A New Dictionary of Birds;* Nelson.

Tottenham, K. (1963). *The Pan Book of Home Pets;* Pan Books.

Turner, E. L. (1935). *Every Garden a Bird Sanctuary;* Witherby.

Vedel, H. and Lange, J. (1960). *Trees and Bushes;* Methuen.

Witherby, H. F., *et al.* (rev. edn. 1952). *The Handbook of British Birds* (5 vols); Witherby.

Acknowledgements

My grateful thanks go to Mary Blair, Tom Edridge, Elaine and H. G. Hurrell, R. M. Lockley, Winwood Reade and E. H. Ware for ploughing through the first draft of this book and offering so much useful advice. David St John Thomas encouraged me to start; hundreds of BBC Spotlight viewers in the West Country forced me to continue by asking questions, instead of answering them as I had requested. Chris Mead and David Wilson of the British Trust for Ornithology and Frank Hamilton and John Taunton of the Royal Society for the Protection of Birds have been most helpful. Many friends have encouraged me with good ideas and corrections; some have even valiantly tried to improve my grammar, but the mistakes that remain are all my own work.

T.S.

Spring, 1965.
North Minack,
Porthcurno,
Cornwall.

Index

Acorns, 43
Adder, 64
Aegithalos caudatus, 86
Alcedo atthis, 77
Aldrin, 60
Almond, 43
Anas platyrhynchos, 69
Animal welfare societies, 110
Anthills, 47
Anti-freeze, 22
Antirrhinum, 18
Anthus spinoletta, 93
Ants, 61
Ant's eggs, 45
Ant's pupae, 45
Ant, Wood, 47
Aphid, 14, 17, 63
Apples, 45
Apus apus, 77
Arenaria interpres, 73
Athene noctua, 76

Bacon, 43
Bananas, 45
Barbary, 15
Basket, Scrap, 49
Bath, Bird, 21
Bath, Dust, 24–5
Batten, H. Mortimer, 51
Bee, 61
Beech, 28
Beech-mast, 43
Beetle, Great Diving, 24
Berberis aggregata, 16
B. darwinii, 15
B. vulgaris, 15
B. wilsonae, 16
Berries, 43
BHC, 60–1
Birdcage, 32
Bird Life, 110
Birds, 110
Bird population, 41
Bird-pudding, 43, 99

Bird Study, 110
Bird tables, 47–9
Blackberries, 43
Blackbird, 34, 52, 89, 104, 105, 106
Blackcap, 91, 104, 106
Blackfly, 61
Blackthorn, 16
Bones, Meat, 43
Bostik, 34
Brambles, 28
Branta canadensis, 70
Brazil nuts, 44, 51
Bread, 43
Bread scraps, 42
British Birds, 111
British Ornithologists' Union, The, 110
British Trust for Ornithology, The, 40, 106, 110
BTO News, 110
Bullfinch, 95, 104, 106
Bunting, Reed, 29
  Yellow, *see* Yellowhammer

Cake, 43
Callitriche autumnalis, 23
Carduelis carduelis, 95
Casualties, 108
Cat, 36, 48, 57–8
Caterpillars, 61
Cedar, 34
Certhia familiaris, 87
Chaffinch, 96, 104, 106
Cheese, 44
Chemical weedkillers and pesticides, 59–61
Cherry, Wild, 43
Chestnut, Horse, 43
Chestnut, Sweet, 43
Chestnuts, 51
Children's Hour, 51
China Aster, 18
Chlordane, 60–1

Chloris chloris, 94
Clent House Gardens, 102
Coccothraustes coccothraustes, 94
Coconut, 44–5, 51
 as nest site, 31
Cohen, Edwin, 40
Columba livia, 74
C. oenas, 74
C. palumbus, 75
Concrete pool, 23
Conkers, 43
Coombs, E. W. Ltd., 100
Cooper's insecticides, 25, 39, 66, 67
Cormorant, 38
Corn, 45
Cornflower, 18
Corvus frugilegus, 81
C. monedula, 82
Corylus avellana, 15
Cosmos, 18
Cotoneaster, 16
Cotoneaster buxifolia, 16
C. dammeri, 16
C. francheti, 16
C. horizontalis, 16
C. integerrima, 16
C. lactea, 16
C. prostrata, 16
C. rotundifolia, 16
C. simonsii, 16
Council for Nature, The, 111
Crab-apple, 14, 43
Crataegus monogyna, 16
Creeper, Tree, 87, 104, 105, 106
Crossbill, 96, 104, 106
Crows, 49
Cygnus olor, 70

DDT, 60–1
Delichon urbica, 80
Dendrocopus major, 79
D. minor, 79
Derris, 61
Devon hedgerow, 14
Dieldrin, 60
Dove, Collared, 75, 104, 106
 Ring, 75
 Rock, 74, 106
 Stock, 74, 105, 106
Dovecote, 31

Drabble, Phil, 58
Dragonflies, 63
Duck, Wild, *see* Mallard
Dunnock, 28, 92, 104, 106
Dytiscus marginalis, 24

Earthworm, 13
Elder, 17, 43
Eleocharis acicularis, 23
Embiriza citrinella, 96
Endosulfan, 60
Endrin, 60
Erithacus rubecula, 90
Euonymus europaeus, 17
Evergreens, 14–15
Exhausted birds, 108

Falco tinnunculus, 71
Fat, 43
Fauna Preservation Society, The, 111
Feathers, *see* Plumage
Fence, Wire, 58
Fieldfare, 43, 88, 104, 106
Finches, 50
Fish, 61
Flea beetles, 61
Flycatcher, 28
Flycatcher, Pied, 92, 105, 106
Flycatcher, Spotted, 92, 105, 106
Forget-me-not, 18
Fringilla coelebs, 96
Fruit, 45

Galapagos Islands, 38
Gallinula chloropus, 72
Garrulus glandarius, 83
Gentles, 45
Glycerine, 22
Gnat, 24
Goldcrest, 91, 104, 106
Goldfinch, 28, 95, 104, 106
Goldfish, 24
Goose, Canada, 29, 70, 104, 106
Gorse, 28
Grapefruit, 45
Grapes, 45
Greenfinch, 94, 104, 106
Greenfly, 61
Greenrigg Works, 100, 102

Ground feeding stations, 52
Guelder rose, 17
Gull, Black-headed, 73, 104, 106
  Herring, 27, 73, 104, 106

Haith, John E. Ltd., 100
Hawfinch, 94, 104, 106
Hawthorn, 14, 16, 28, 58
Haws, 43
Hazel, 15, 28, 43
  nuts, 43, 51
Hedera helix, 17
Hedge, 58
Hedges, as nest sites, 28
Hedgehog, 23, 64–8
  nestbox, 66–8
Hedgerow, 14
Hemp, 45
Henry Doubleday Research Association, 61, 66, 110
Heron, 22, 24
Hills, Lawrence D., 61
Hirundo rustica, 80
Hole making, 29
Holly, 16, 28, 58
Honeysuckle, 17, 31
Hoopoe, 32, 77–8, 106
Hopper, Seed, 49–50
Hottonia palustris, 23

Ibis, The, 110
Ice, 22
Ilex aquifolium, 16
I. Golden King, 17
I. Madame Briot, 17
Injured birds, 109
Insects, 63
Insecticide 25, 59–61, 66
International Council for Bird Preservation, The, 110
International Paint Co., 32
International Union for Conservation of Nature, 111
Isoetes lacustris, 23
Ivy, 17

Jackdaw, 38, 82, 104, 105, 106
  nest material, 38
Jay, 59, 83, 104, 106
Jynx torquilla, 79

Kestrel, 33, 71, 106
Kettle for robin's nest, 32
Kingfisher, 22, 77, 104, 106
Kitchen scraps, 43–4
Knapweed, 18, 43

Ladybirds, 63
Larch cones, 43
Larus argentatus, 73
L. ridibundus, 73
Law, Birds and the, 112
Lawn, 13
Life-spans of wild birds, 106
Lime, 17
Lindane, 60, 61
Linden, 17
Linnet, 28
Longevity, 106
Lonicera periclymenum, 17
Loxia curvirostra, 96

Maize, 45
Magpie, 59, 82, 104, 106
Malathion, 61
Mallard, 69, 104, 106
Martin, House, 80, 105, 106
Martin, Sand, 81, 105, 106
Mealworms, 45
Mealworm culture, 99–100
Meat, 43
Melon, 44
Mice, 48
Middle Wallop, 32
Milk, 45
Millet, 45
Ministry of Agriculture, Fisheries and Food, 60, 61
Minnow, 24
Moorhen, 52, 72, 104, 106
Mosquito, 24
Motacilla alba, 93
Mountain Ash, 16
Muscicapa hypoleuca, 92
M. striata, 92

Natural food, 42–3
Newt, 24
Nestbox, 31–40
  construction, 33–6
  main types, 33–4
  numbers, 37

Nestbox – contd.
  priming, 37
  rustic, 34
  when to erect, 36
Nestboxes, pamphlet, 40
Nest material, 38
Nest sites, 27–31
Nettle, 18, 43
Newton Ferrers, 32
Nicotine, 61
Noah, 31
Nut, Brazil, 51
Nuts, 43, 50–1
Nuthatch, 29, 44, 51, 86, 104,
    105, 106

Oats, 45
'Oiling', 20
Oranges, 45
Organo-chlorine pesticides, 59,
    60, 68
Orphaned birds, 108
Owl, Barn, 76, 105, 106
    Little, 76, 105, 106
    Tawny, 76–7, 105, 106

Parasites, 39
Parus ater, 84
P. atricapillus, 85
P. caeruleus, 84
P. cristatus, 85
P. major, 83
P. palustris, 85
Passer domesticus, 97
P. montanus, 97
PDSA, 109
Peanuts, 44, 50
Peanut butter, 51
Perfumes against pests, 61
Pest control without poisons, 61
Pesticides, 61
Phasianus colchicus, 72
Pheasant, 72, 104, 106
Phoenicurus ochruros, 90
P. phoenicurus, 89–90
Pica pica, 82
Picus viridis, 78
Pigeon, Domestic, 74–5
    Feral, 75, 104
    Racing, 32
    Wood, 75, 104, 106
Pigeon lofts, 31–2

Pine cones, 43
Pipit, Rock, 93, 104, 106
Plumage, 19–21
Poisons, 59–61
Pond, 22–4
Pool, 22
Poppy, Common field, 18
Porridge, 45
Potato, 43
Predators, 57–9
Primrose, Evening, 18
Privet hawk-moth, 18
Protection of Birds Act, 112
Prunella modularis, 92
Pyrethrins, 61
Pyrethrum, 61
Pyrrhula pyrrhula, 95

Quillwort, 23

Rain, 34
Ragwort, 18, 43
Rats, 48, 58–9
Rat traps, 59
Recipes, 99
Recordings, Birdsong, 113
Redstart, 89–90, 105, 106
    Black, 90, 106
Redwing, 89, 104, 106
Regulus regulus, 91
Rhothane, 60
Rice, 45
Riparia riparia, 81
Robin, 30, 34, 45, 90–1, 104,
    105, 107
Rook, 49, 81, 104, 107
Rowan, 16, 43
Royal Society for the Protec-
    tion of Birds, 49, 50, 110
    and bird law, 112
    gramophone records, 113
    products, 101
RSPCA, 109, 112

Sagittaria graminea, 23
Sambucus nigra, 17
Sawfly, 61
Scabious, 18
Scrap baskets, 49
Seed, Canary, 45
    Mixed wild bird, 45
    Sunflower, 45

Seed-hopper, 49–50
Selection problems, 53
Shed, 31
Shove, Lawrence C., 113
Sitta europae, 86
Sloes, 43
Snail, 31
  Water, 24
Snake, Grass, 23
Snowball bush, 17
Society for the Promotion o
  Nature Reserves, 111
Sorbus aucuparia, 16
S. vilmorinii, 16
Sparrows, 52, 53
Sparrows, Hedge, *see* Dunnock
  House, 97, 104, 105, 107
  nest composition, 38
  Tree, 97, 104, 105, 107
Sparrowhawk, 57
Spiders, 63
Spindle, 17
Spray, 61
Spring, 54
Squirrel, Grey, 38, 57, 59
Starling, 29, 34, 38, 53, 93–4,
  104, 105, 107
Stickleback, 24
Stilton, 44
Stork, 33
Stormcock, *see* Thrush, Mistle
Streptopelia decaocto, 75
Strix aluco, 76–7
Sturnus vulgaris, 93–4
Suet, 45
  stick, 52
Sunflower, 18
Suppliers of bird furniture, etc.
  101, 102
Swallow, 19, 30, 80, 105
Swan, Mute, 27, 70, 104, 107
  on raft, 32
Swift, 19, 77, 105, 107
Swoop, 44
Sylvia atricapilla, 91

Table, Bird, 47–52
Taxus baccata, 15
Teazle, 18, 43
Thistle, 18, 43
Thrips, 61, 63
Thrush, 53

Thrush, Mistle, 88, 104, 107
  Song, 88, 104, 107
Tilia cordata, 17
Tillaea recurva, 23
Tits, 50–1
Tit, Blue, 27, 37, 84, 104, 105,
  107
  Coal, 84, 104, 105, 107
  Crested, 85, 107
  Great, 30, 83, 104, 105, 107
  Long-tailed, 86, 104, 107
  Marsh, 85, 104, 105, 107
  Willow, 85, 104, 105, 107
Tit-bell, 51
Toad, 63–4
Tomatoes, 45
Topsoil, 14
Trap, rat, 59
Treatment of casualties, 108
Tree Creeper, *see* Creeper, Tree
Troglodytes troglodytes, 87
Turdus ericetorum, 88
T. merula, 89
T. musicus, 89
T. pilaris, 88
T. viscivorus, 88
Turnstone, 73, 104, 107
Tyto alba, 76

Upupa epops, 77–8

Viburnum opulus, 17
V. compactum, 17

Wagtail, Grey, 30, 107
Wagtail, Pied, 30, 93, 104, 105,
  107
  Sedge, 29
  Reed, 29
Ware, E. H., 48
Warfarin, 59
Water, 19–25
Water-beetle, 24
Waterhen, *see* Moorhen
Water-spider, 24
Water violet, 23
Weeds, 18
Weed-seeds, 43
Wheat-hopper, 53
Whitefly, 61
Whitehorn, 16
Wholefood Ltd., 100

Wildfowl Trust, The, 110
Window-sills, 52
Witherby's sound guide, 113
Woodpecker, 29, 38, 52
    Great Spotted, 43, 79, 104,
        105, 107
    Green, 78, 104, 105, 107
    Lesser Spotted, 79, 104, 107
    enticing to nestbox, 37
Wood, Eric, 100, 102

Wood pigeon, *see* Pigeon, Wood
Worms, 13
Wren, 87, 104, 105, 107
    drinking stick, 24
Wryneck, 79–80, 105, 107

Yellowhammer, 96, 104, 107
Yew, 15, 28
Young Ornithologists' Club,
    110

GAVIN MAXWELL

The House of Elrig   illus. 6/-

The story of the author's childhood and adolescence,
this book shows the vivid impact of the countryside on
a sensitive child.

'Sensitive, brilliantly evocative, with implications far
beyond its matter, this is a book to read, re-read and
keep' Spectator

Ring of Bright Water   illus. 5/-

Camusfeàrna, a remote home in the Scottish Highlands,
a pet otter as intelligent and affectionate as a dog, this
is both a moving and a fascinating account of the
author's homelife.

'A masterpiece... will delight and fascinate even those
most indifferent to animals' The Listener

The Rocks Remain   illus. 5/-

A sequel to 'Ring of Bright Water', this book is packed
with adventure, humour and suspense. And there are
two new otters to join Maxwell, but not quite such
well-behaved ones as Mijbil, the first otter who lived
at Camusfeàrna.

'As beautifully written, as vivid, and as moving as its
predecessor' Guardian

SIR FRANCIS CHICHESTER

ALONG THE CLIPPER WAY 6/-

An anthology of writings about the
nineteenth-century clipper routes to
and from Australia.

'From sunlit blue waters with splashing
dolphin to the stormy Cape Horn, it is
all bold and romantic.' *Times Literary Supplement*

'There is some marvellous writing here, and
the various pieces are stitched together neatly
by the compiler's own comments and
explanations.' *Church Times*

THE LONELY SEA
AND THE SKY 6/-

The autobiography of one of the most
remarkable adventurers of the twentieth
century.

'An astonishing document . . . more than a story
of adventure . . . . it may help and inspire readers
who have nothing in common with the author
himself—people who have no wish to go any
further than a trip round the lighthouse in the
Skylark.' *Sunday Express*

'A remarkable book by a remarkable man.'
                                    Books and Bookmen

A SELECTION OF
POPULAR READING IN PAN

- [ ] **PRIDE AND PREJUDICE** Jane Austen   3/6
- [ ] **INHERITANCE** Phyllis Bentley   7/6
- [ ] **SHOOTING SCRIPT** Gavin Lyall   5/-
- [ ] **WUTHERING HEIGHTS** Emily Brontë   3/6
- [ ] **THE SOUND OF THUNDER** Wilbur A. Smith   6/-
- [ ] **ONE OF OUR SUBMARINES** Edward Young (illus.)   5/-
- [ ] **ROSEMARY'S BABY** Ira Levin   5/-
- [ ] **EAGLE DAY** Richard Collier (illus.)   6/-
- [ ] **THE MAN WITH THE GOLDEN GUN** Ian Fleming   3/6
- [ ] **THE SPY WHO LOVED ME** Ian Fleming   3/6
- [ ] **THE MAGUS** John Fowles   8/6
- [ ] **FRUIT OF THE POPPY** Robert Wilder   5/-

- [ ] **I CAN SEE YOU BUT YOU CAN'T SEE ME**
  Eugene George 5/-
- [ ] **THE ROOM UPSTAIRS** Monica Dickens   5/-
- [ ] **A SENTENCE OF LIFE** Julian Gloag   6/-
- [ ] **ON FORSYTE 'CHANGE** John Galsworthy   5/-
- [ ] **FAR FROM THE MADDING CROWD**
  Thomas Hardy 5/-
- [ ] **THE RELUCTANT WIDOW** Georgette Heyer   5/-
- [ ] **FREDERICA** Georgette Heyer   5/-
- [ ] **STRANGERS ON A TRAIN** Patricia Highsmith   5/-
- [ ] **STORIES MY MOTHER NEVER TOLD ME (Part I)**
  Alfred Hitchcock 3/6
- [ ] **YOUNG BESS** Margaret Irwin   5/-
- [ ] **THE DEEP BLUE GOOD-BYE** John D. MacDonald 3/6
- [ ] **THE LIFE OF IAN FLEMING**
  John Pearson (illus.) 7/6
- [ ] **SHAMELADY** James Mayo   3/6
- [ ] **MADONNA OF THE SEVEN HILLS** Jean Plaidy   5/-
- [ ] **ROUND THE BEND** Nevil Shute   5/
- [ ] **THE BOSTON STRANGLER** Gerold Frank   7/6

Obtainable from all booksellers and newsagents. If you have any difficulty, please send purchase price plus 6d. postage to PO Box 11, Falmouth, Cornwall.

I enclose a cheque/postal order for selected titles ticked above plus 6d. per book to cover packing and postage.

NAME _____

ADDRESS _____

_____